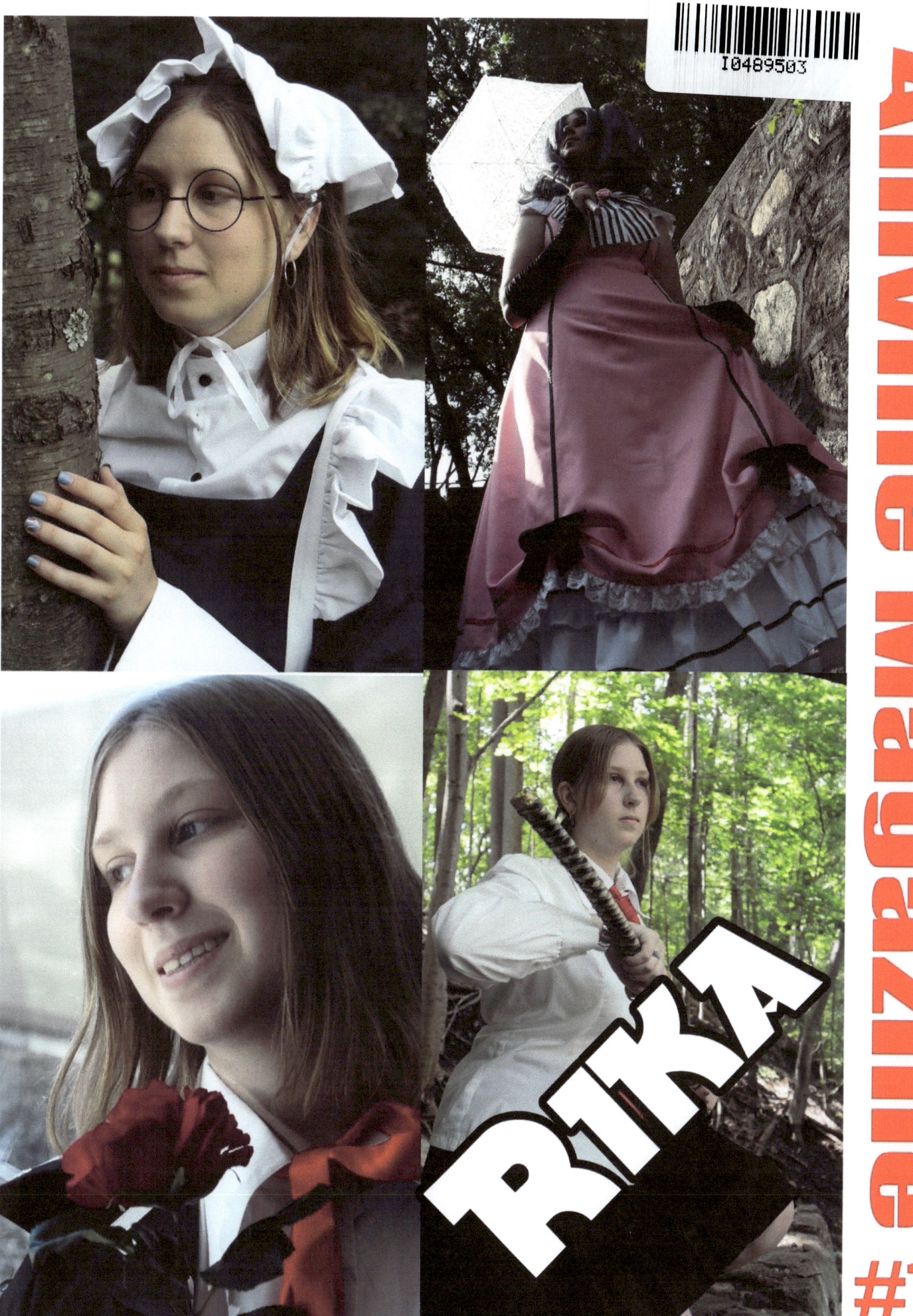

Aniville Magazine #

RIKA

For information about custom editions, special sales, signings, premium,
and corporate purchases please contact:

Sound Impressions (973) 263-0521

Publisher: Sound Impressions
            Attn: Publishing
            PO Box 754
            Boonton, NJ 07005

            http://www.soundimp.net

Model: Rika

Photography By: Jason Koba

Editing & Layout: Jason Koba

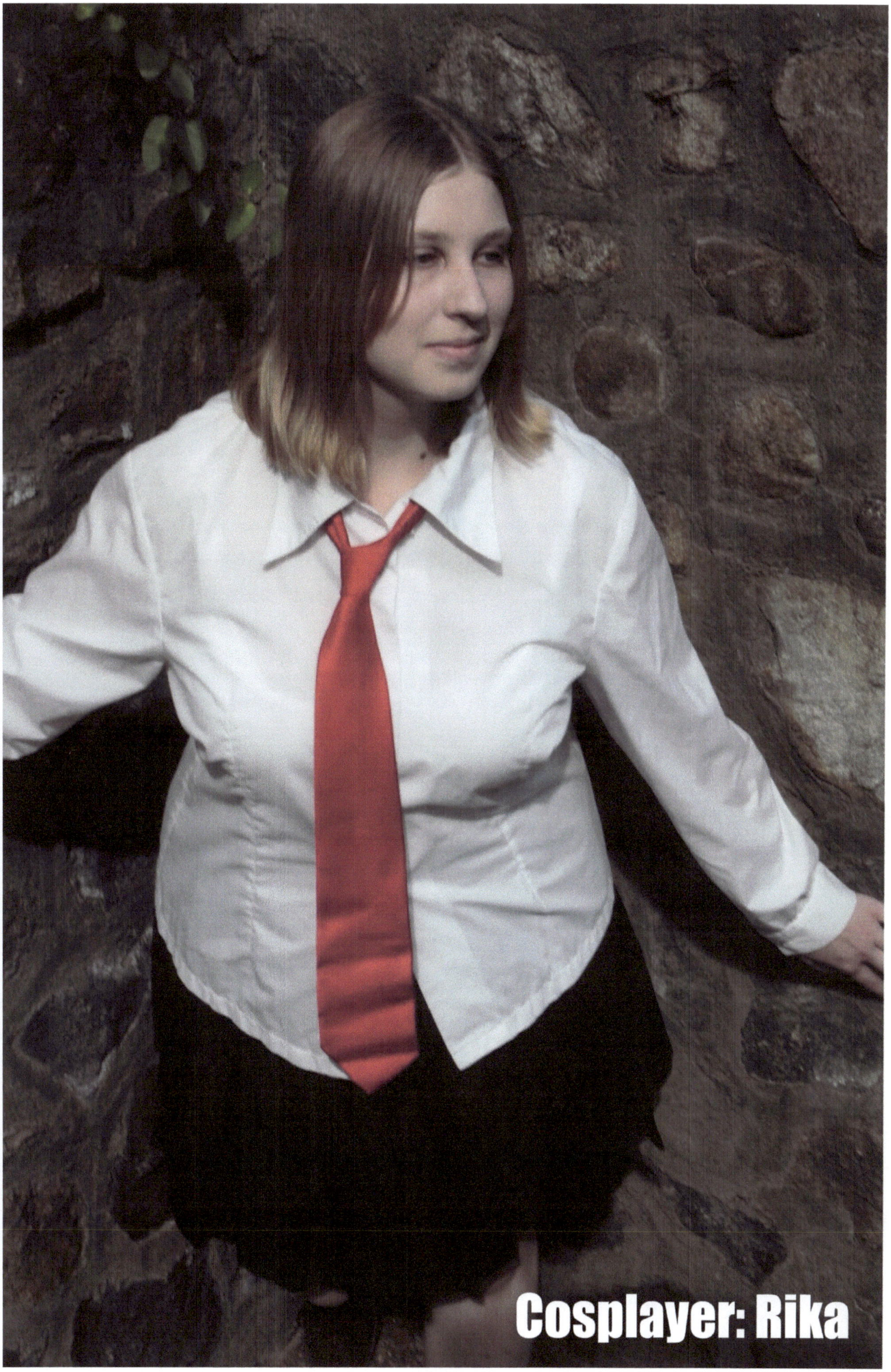

www.aniville.com

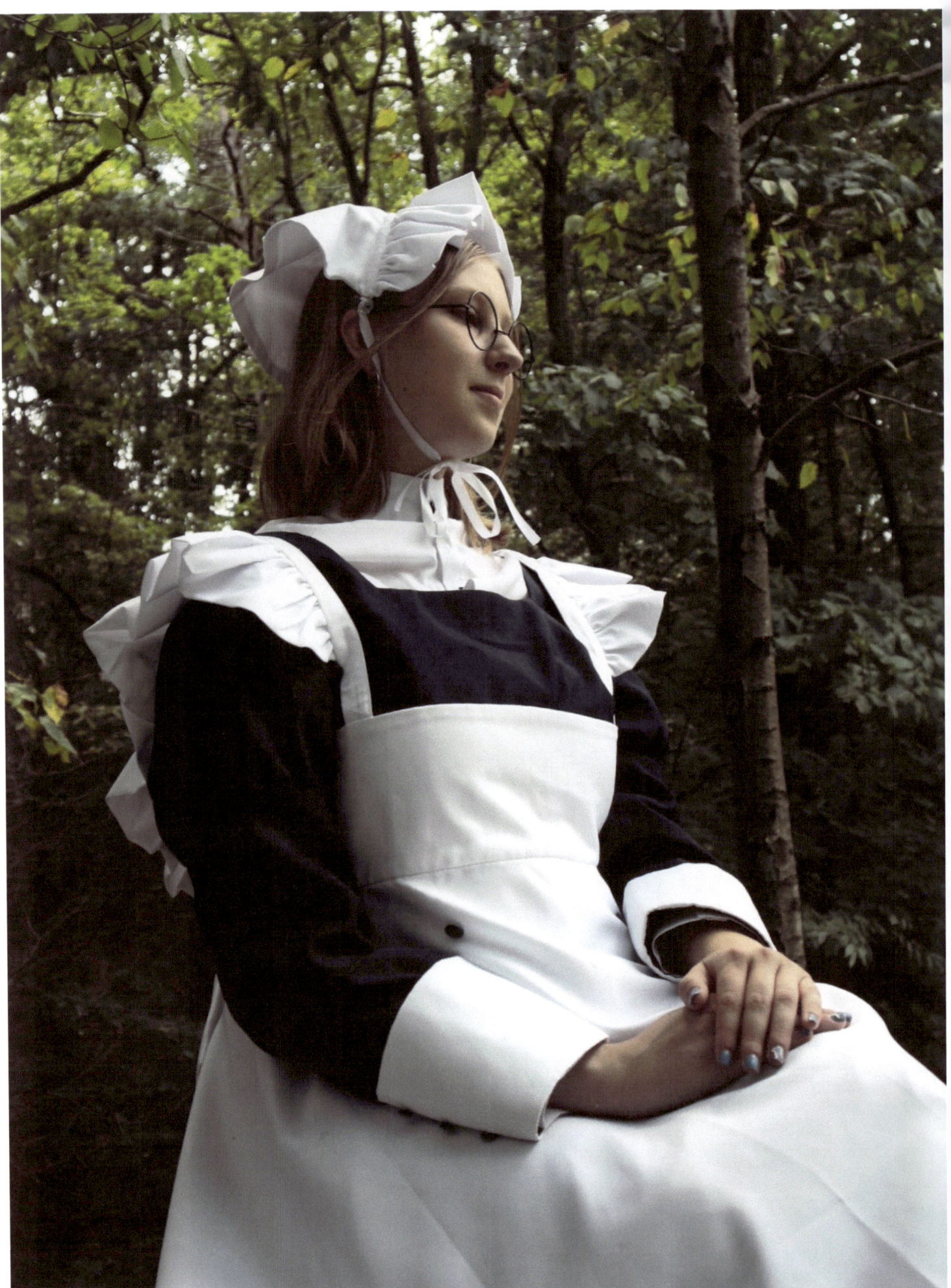

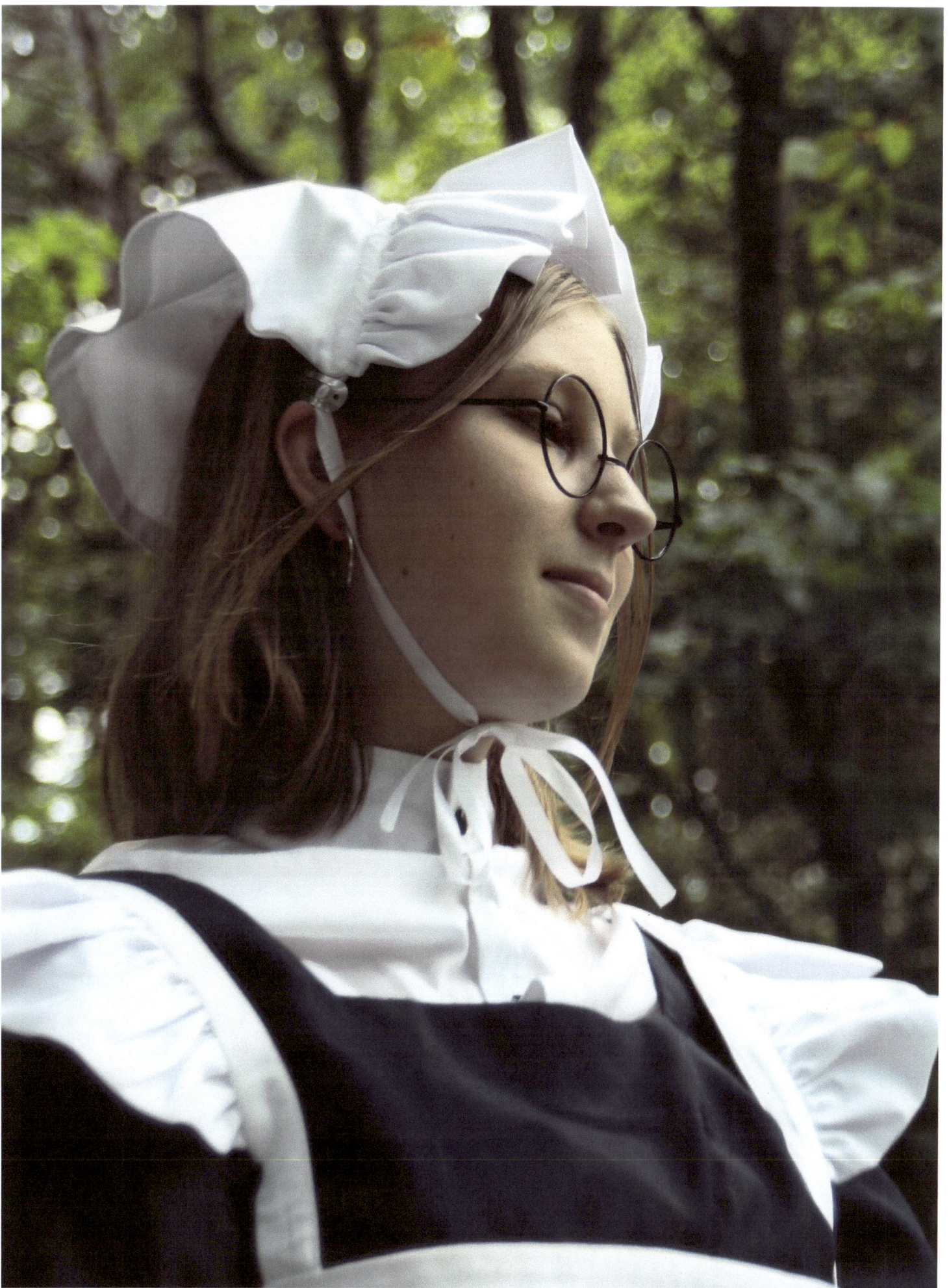

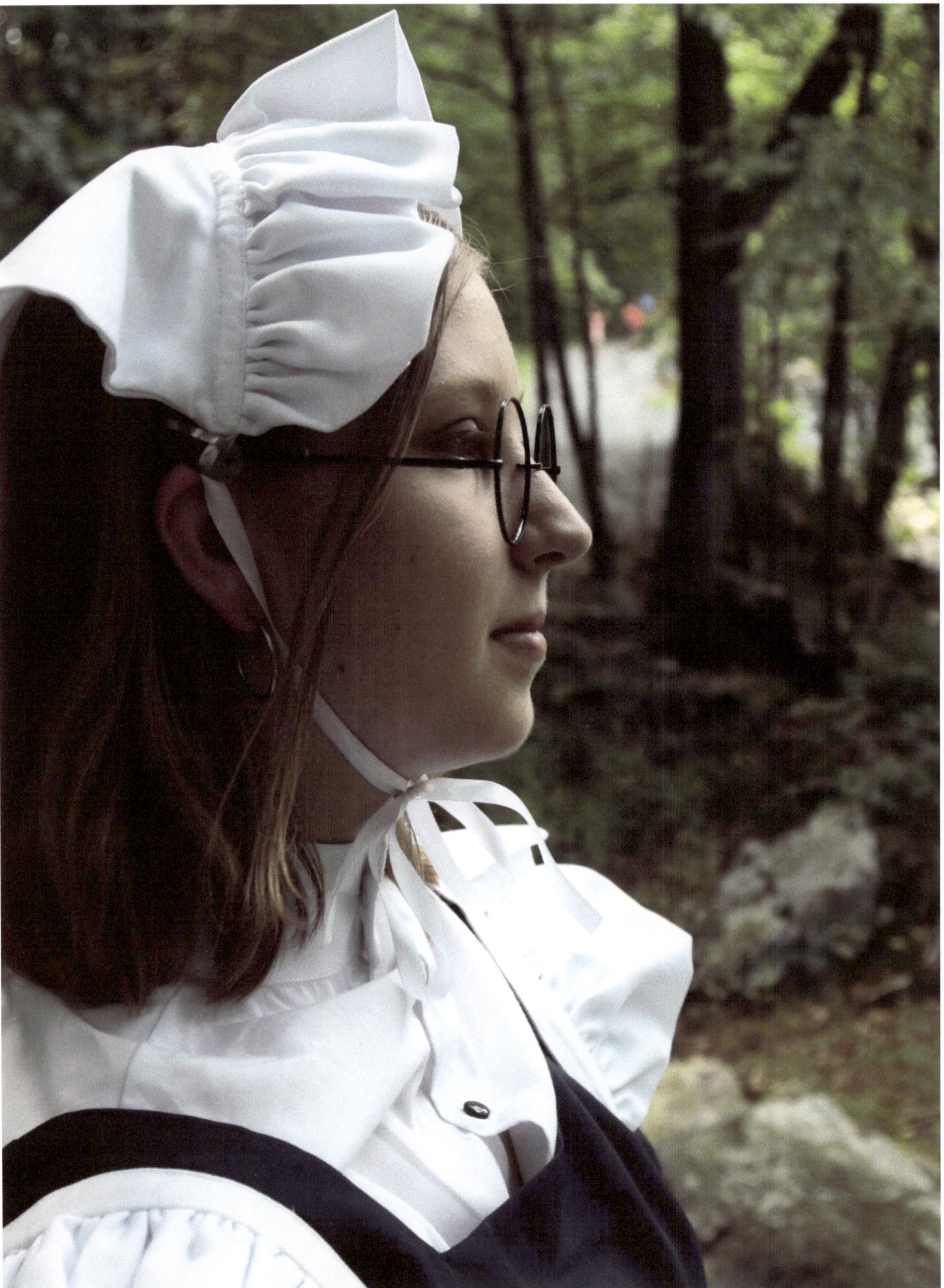

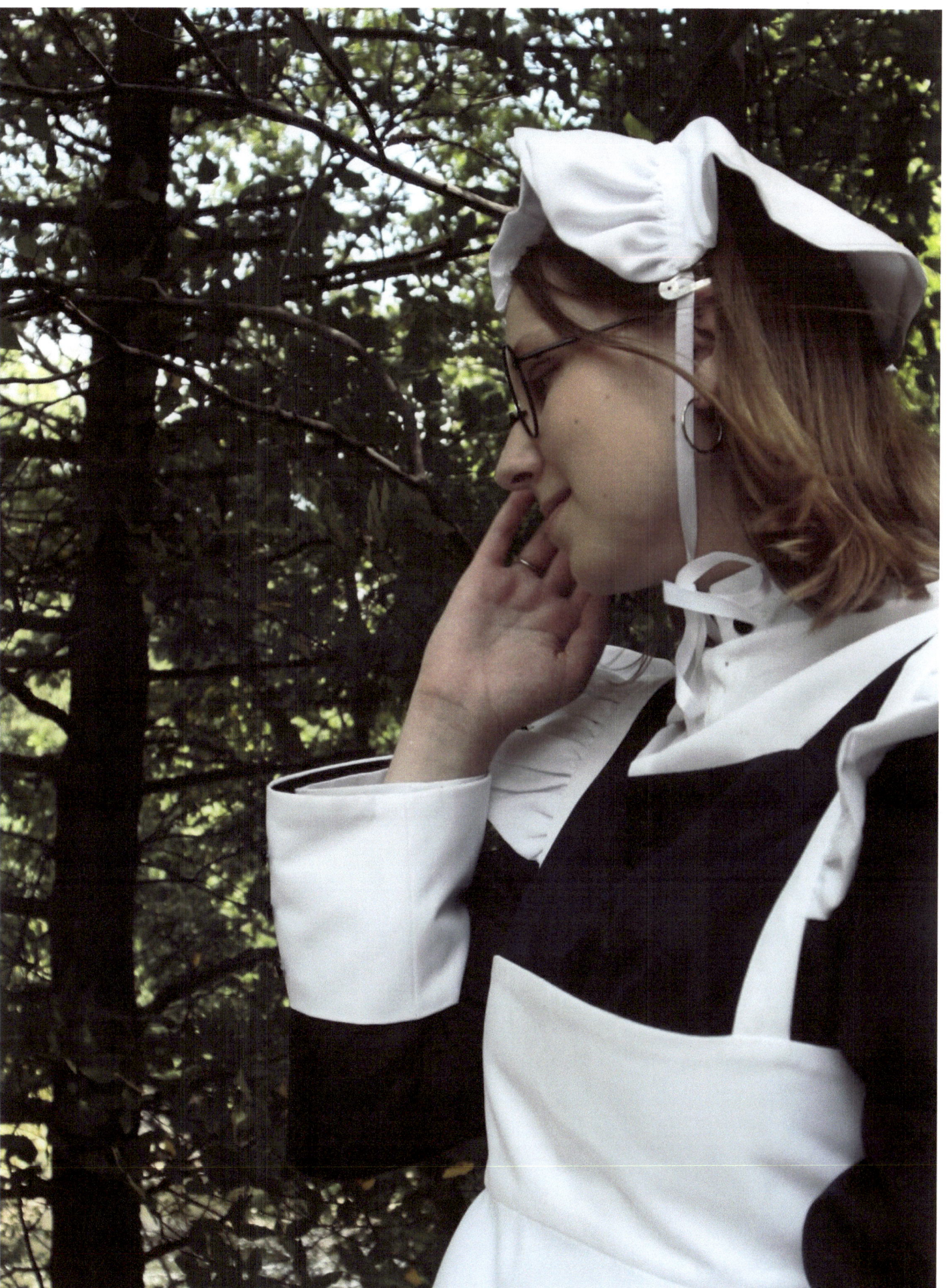

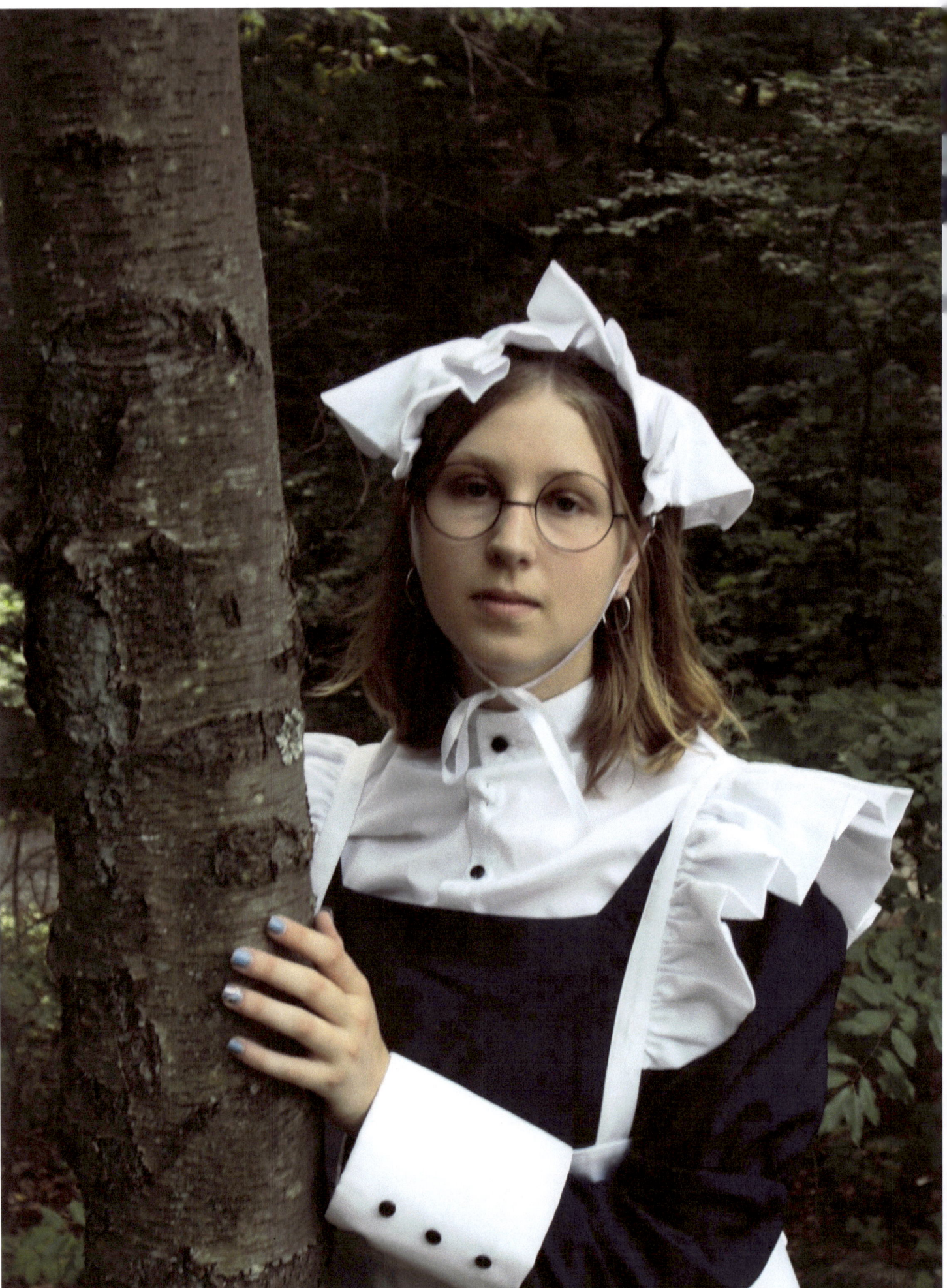

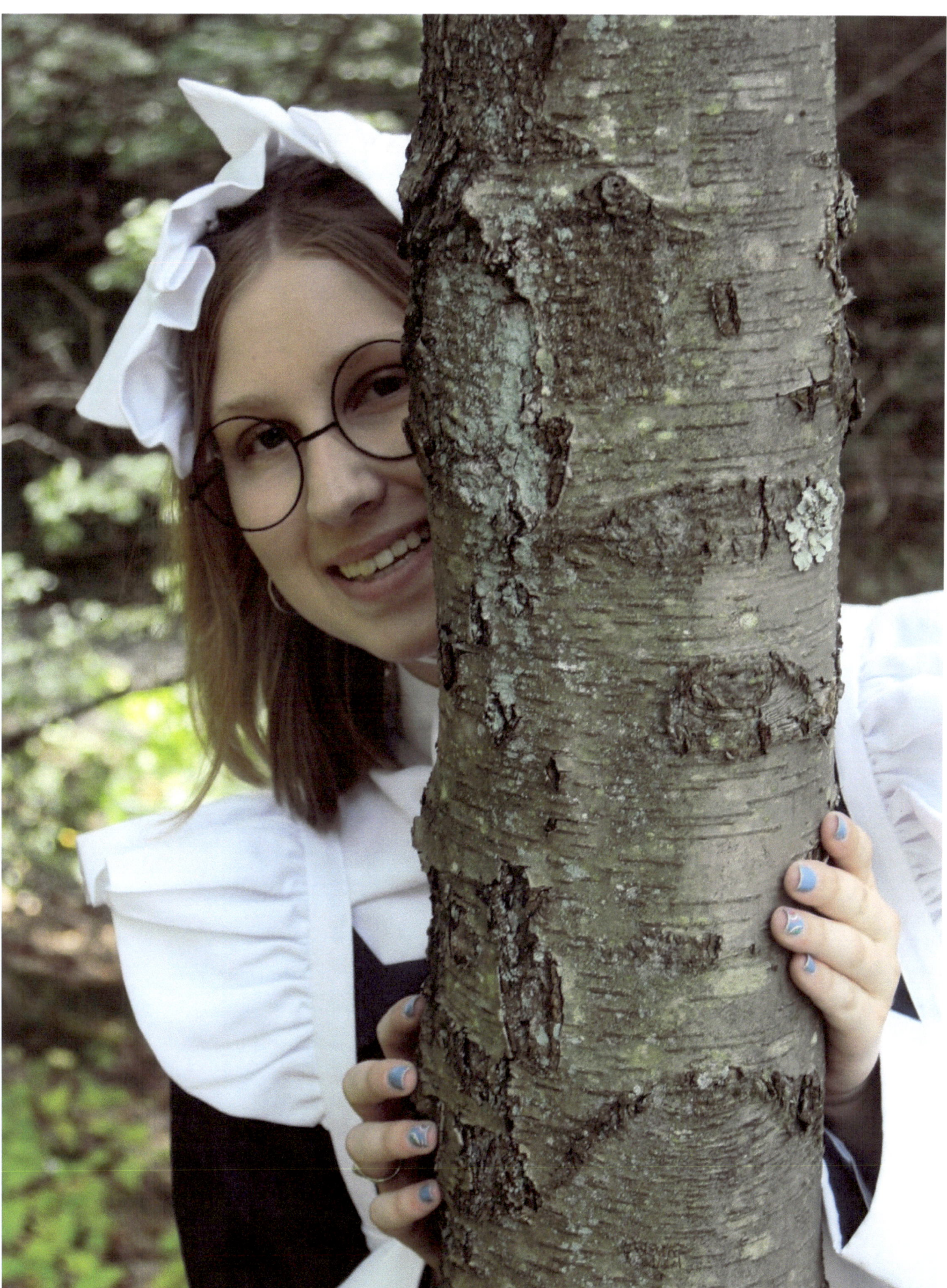

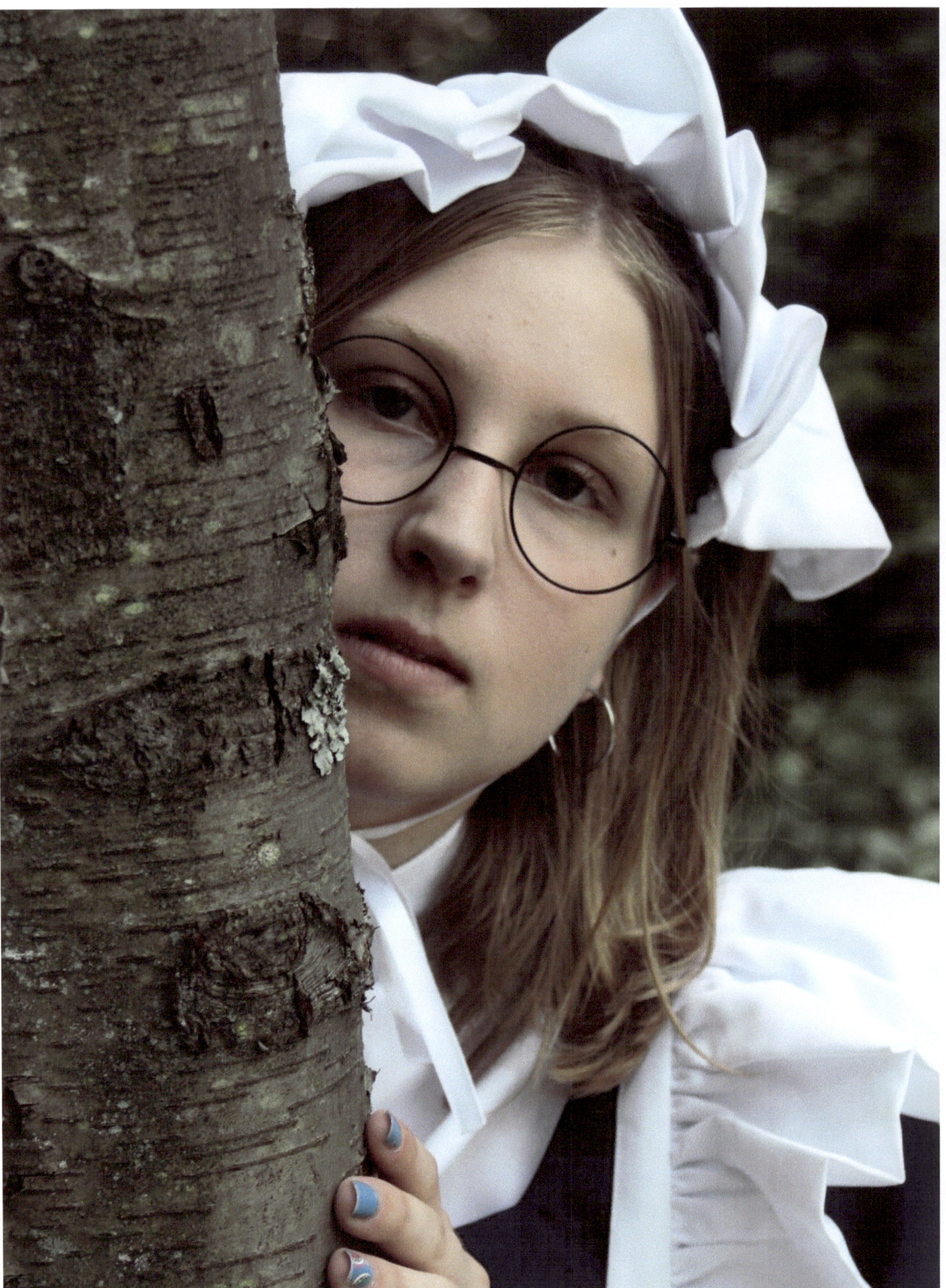

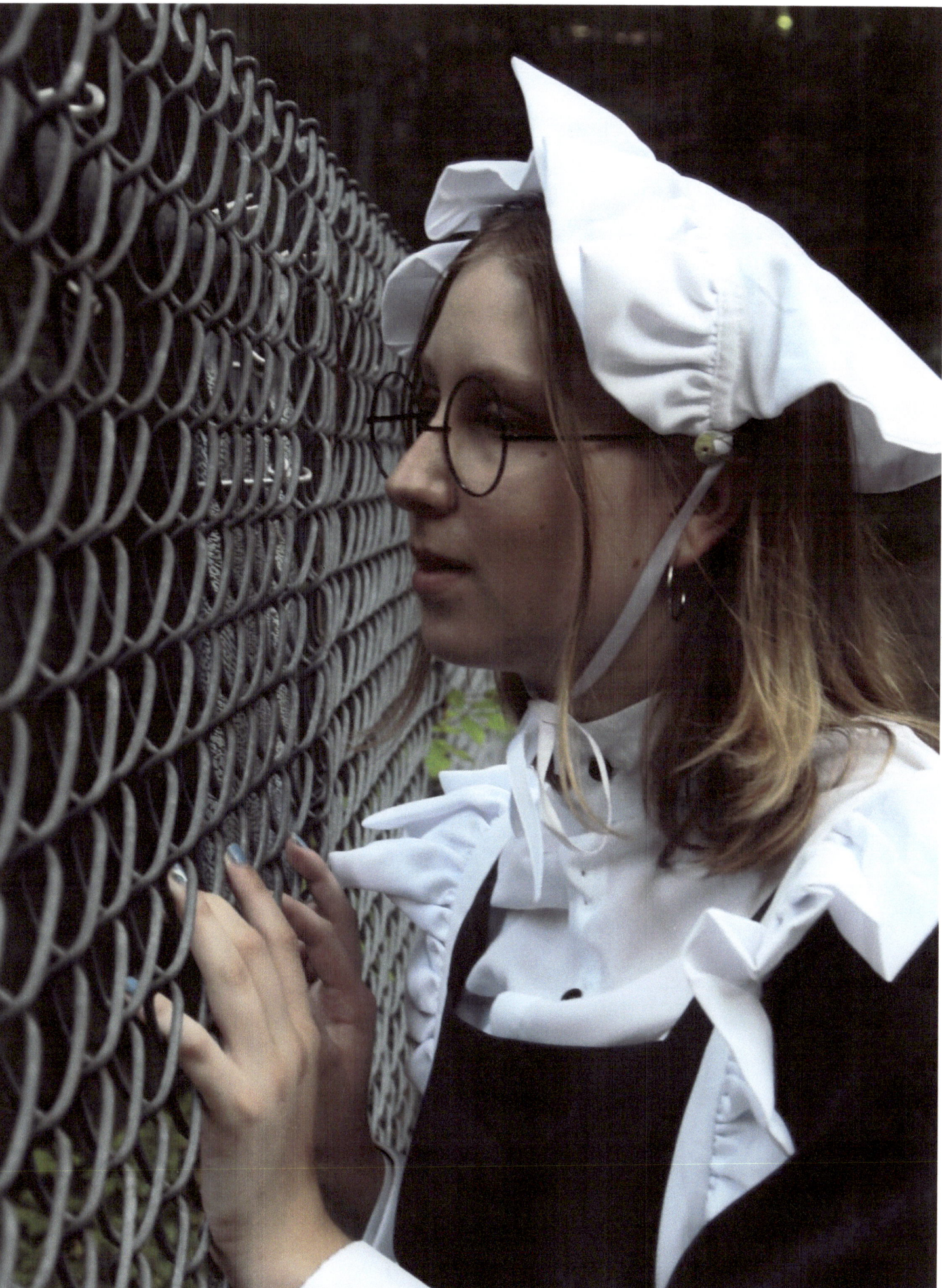

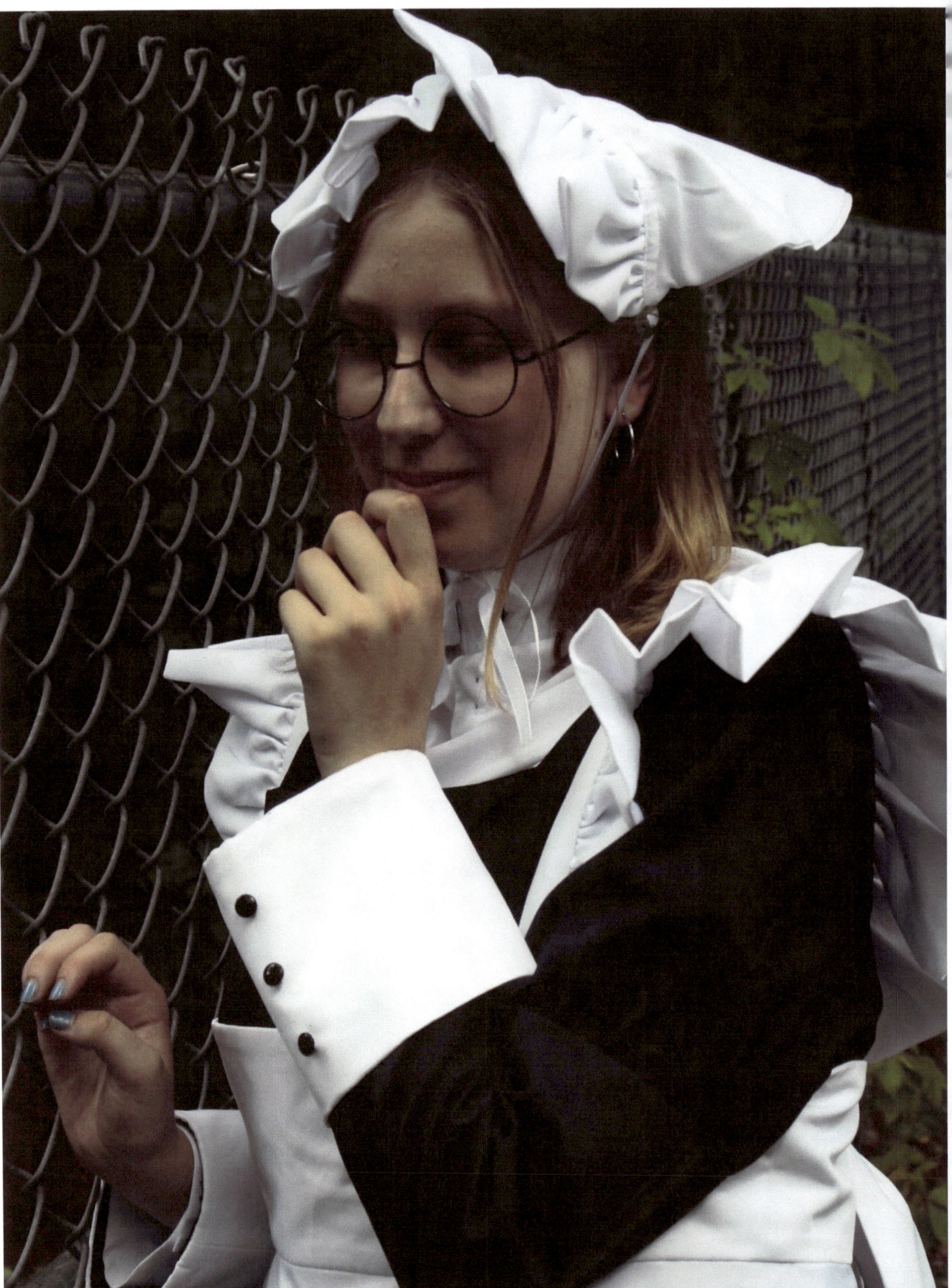

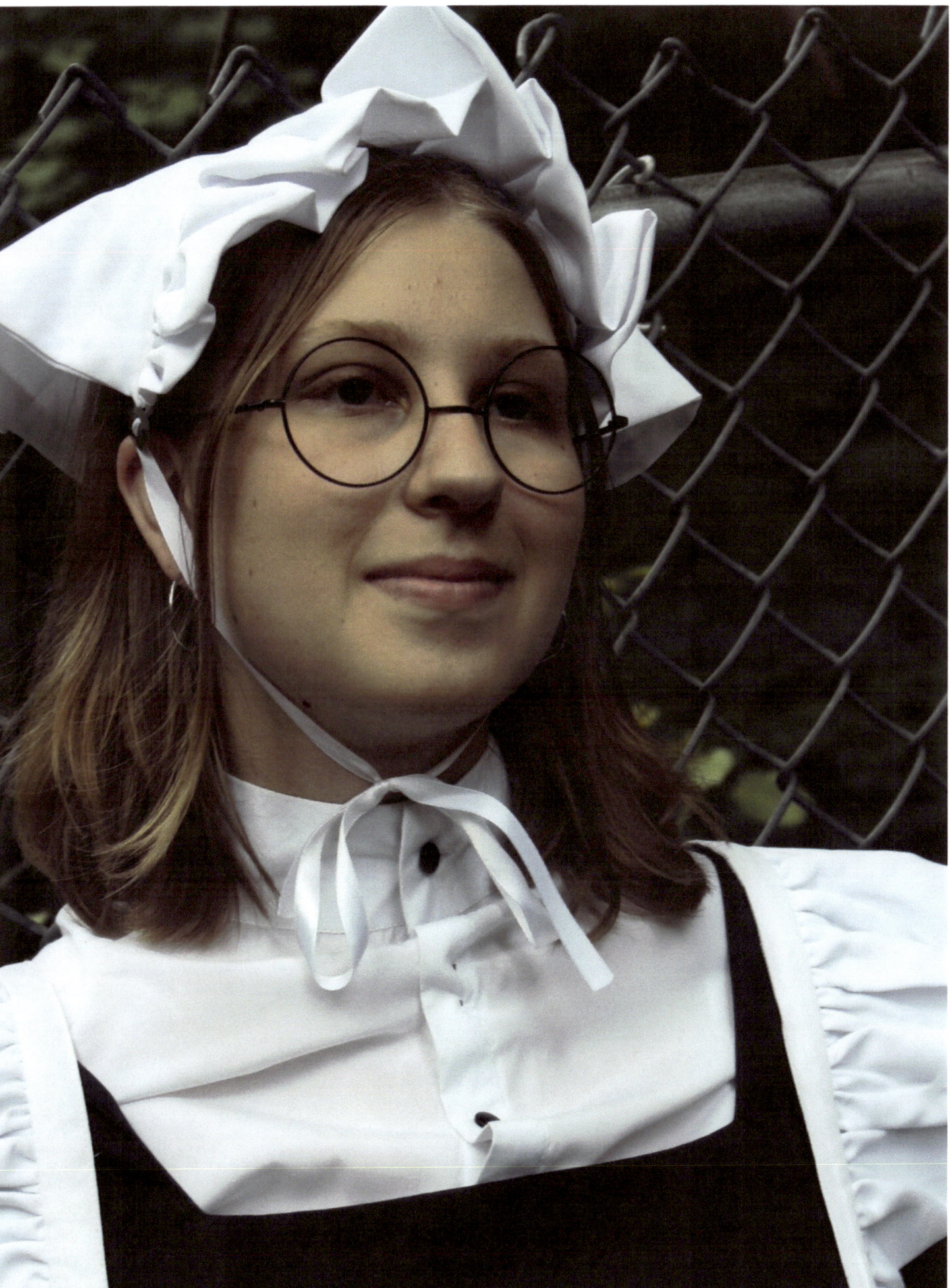

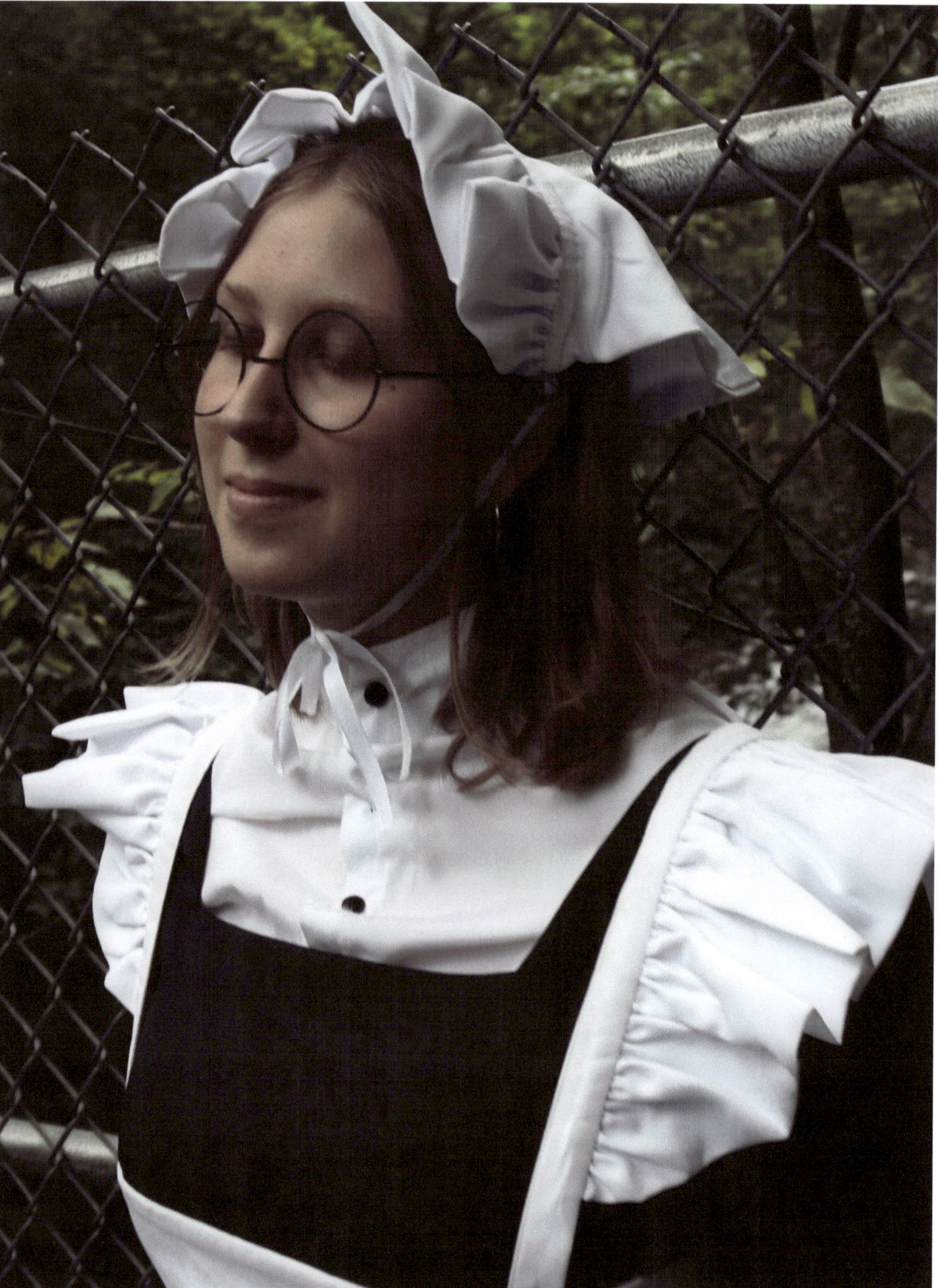

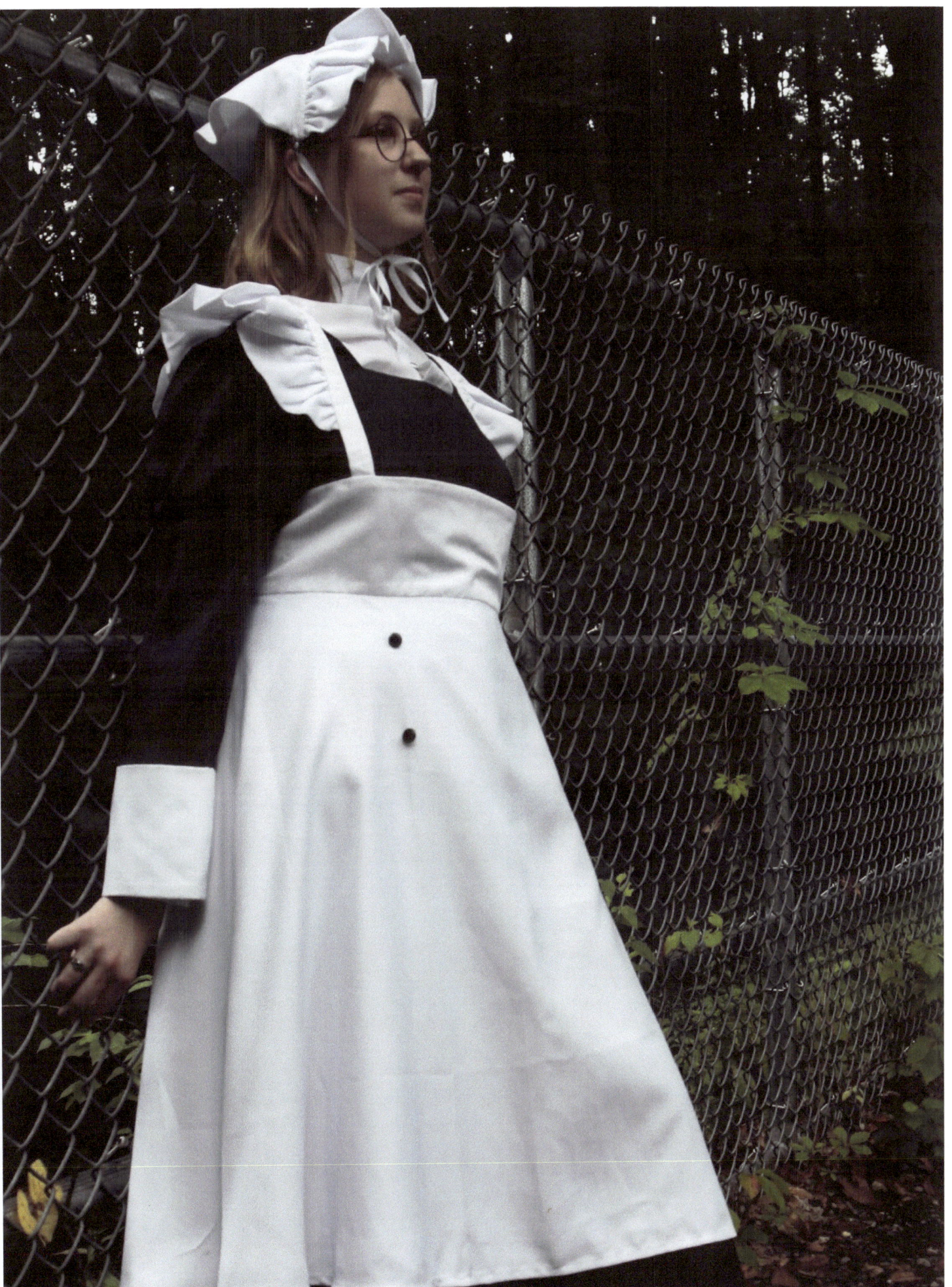

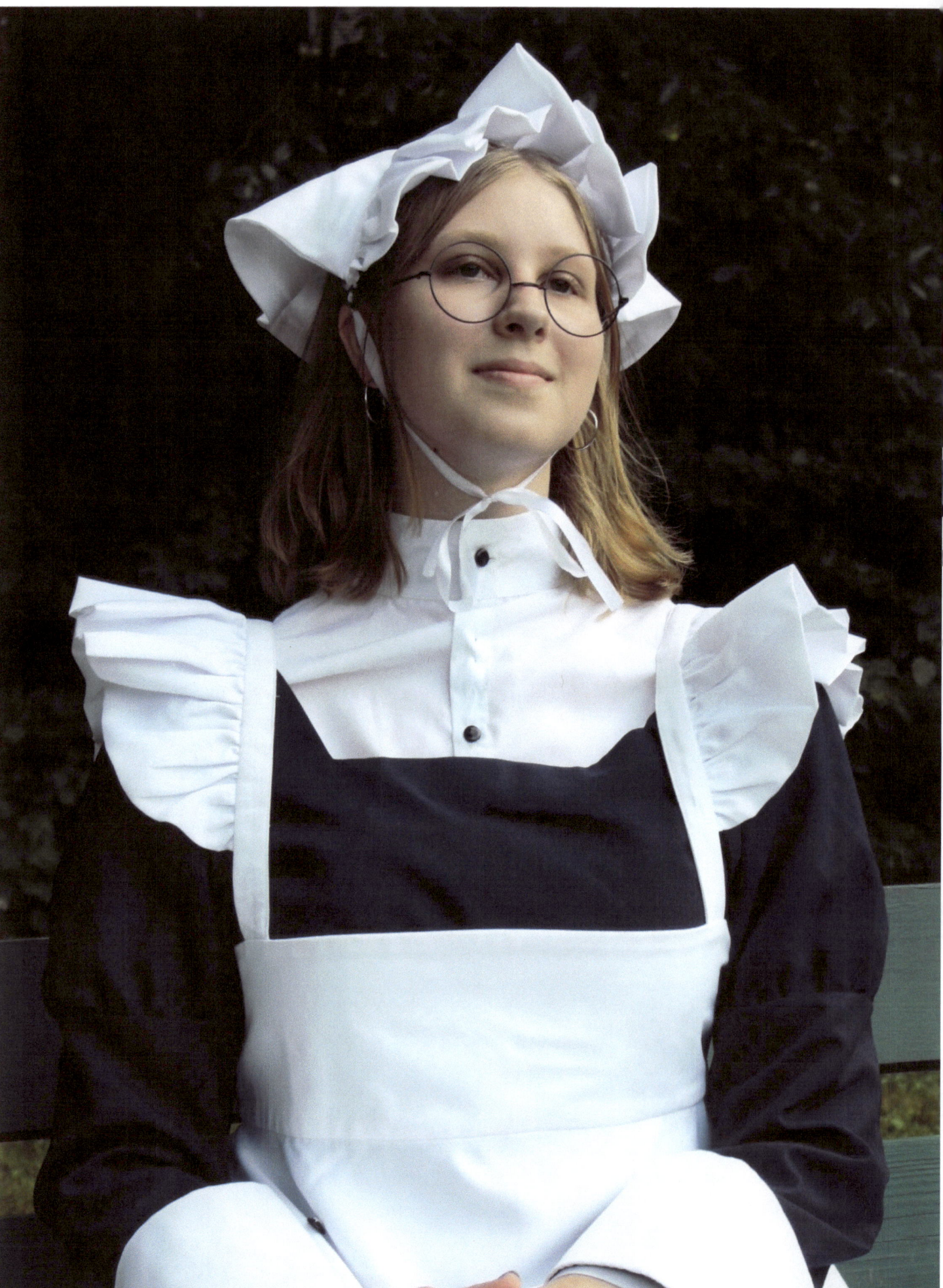

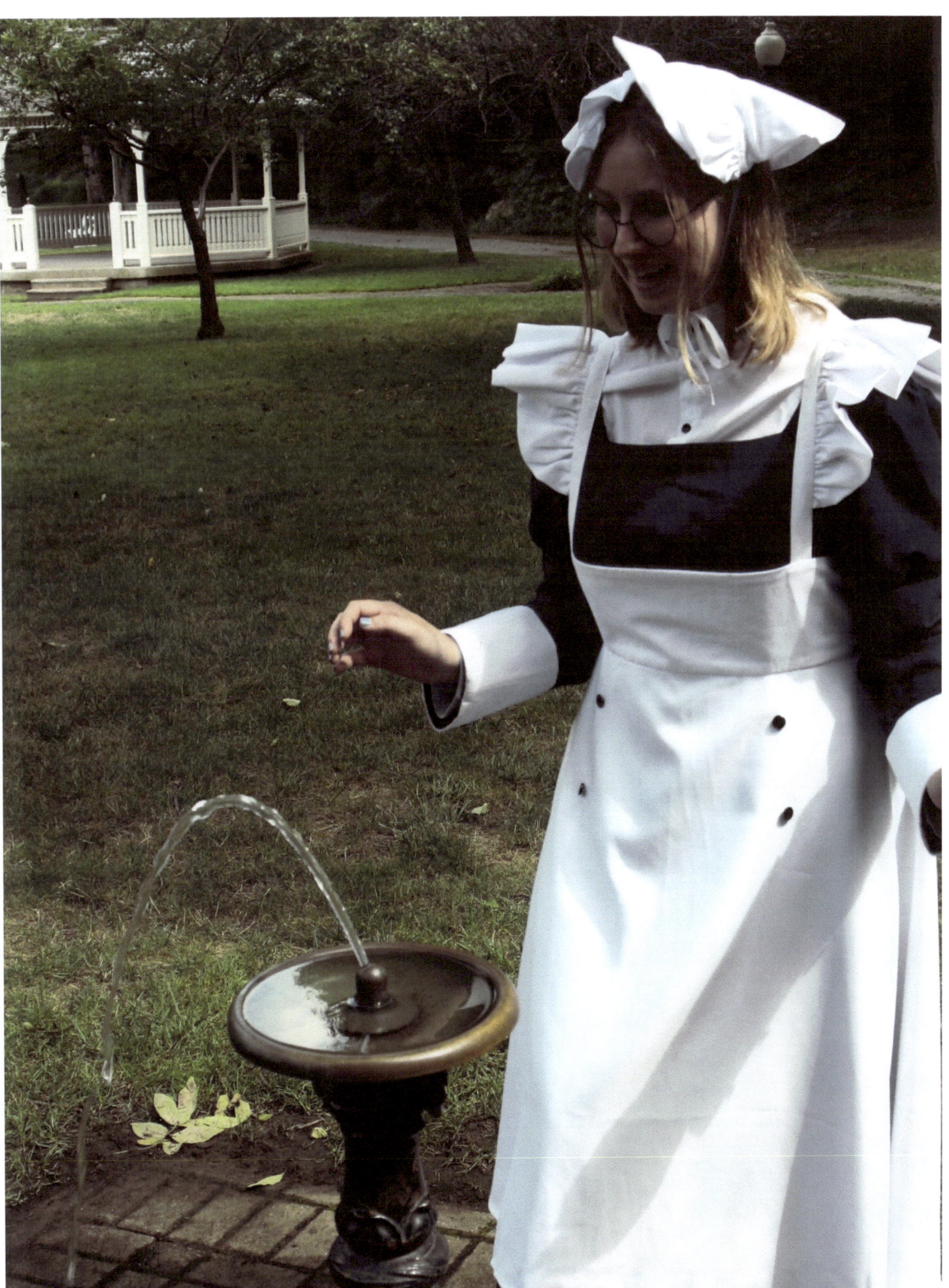

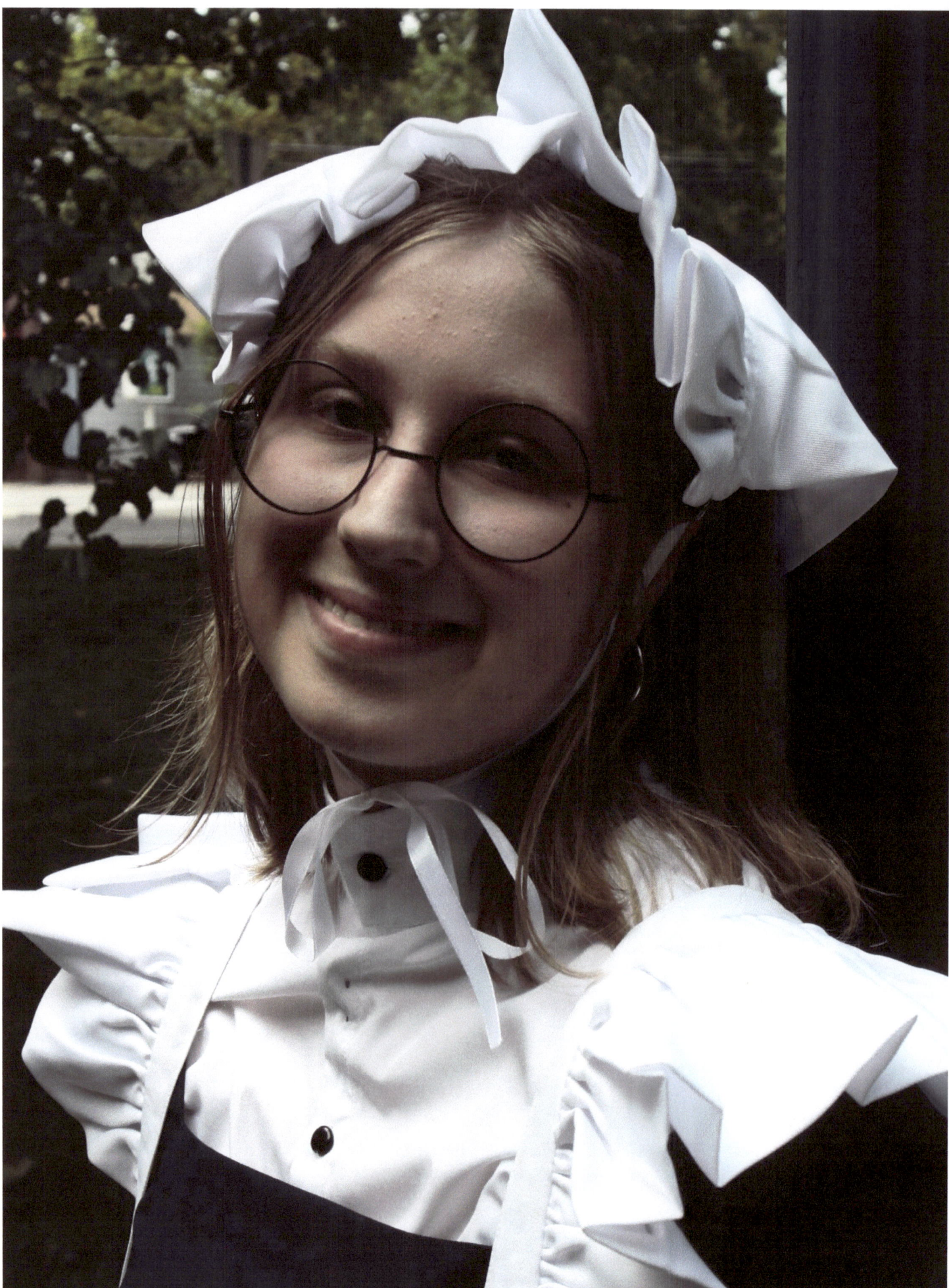

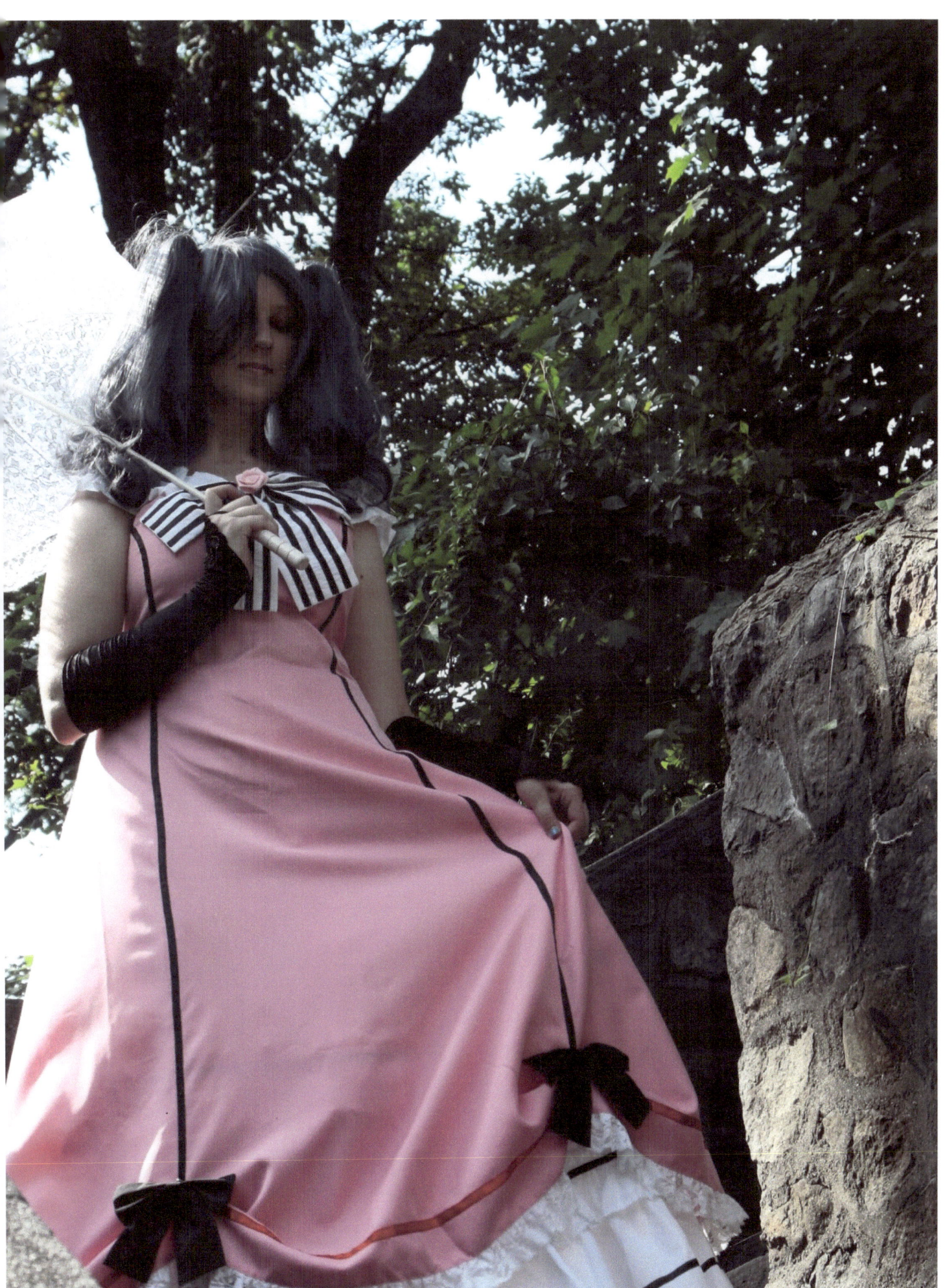

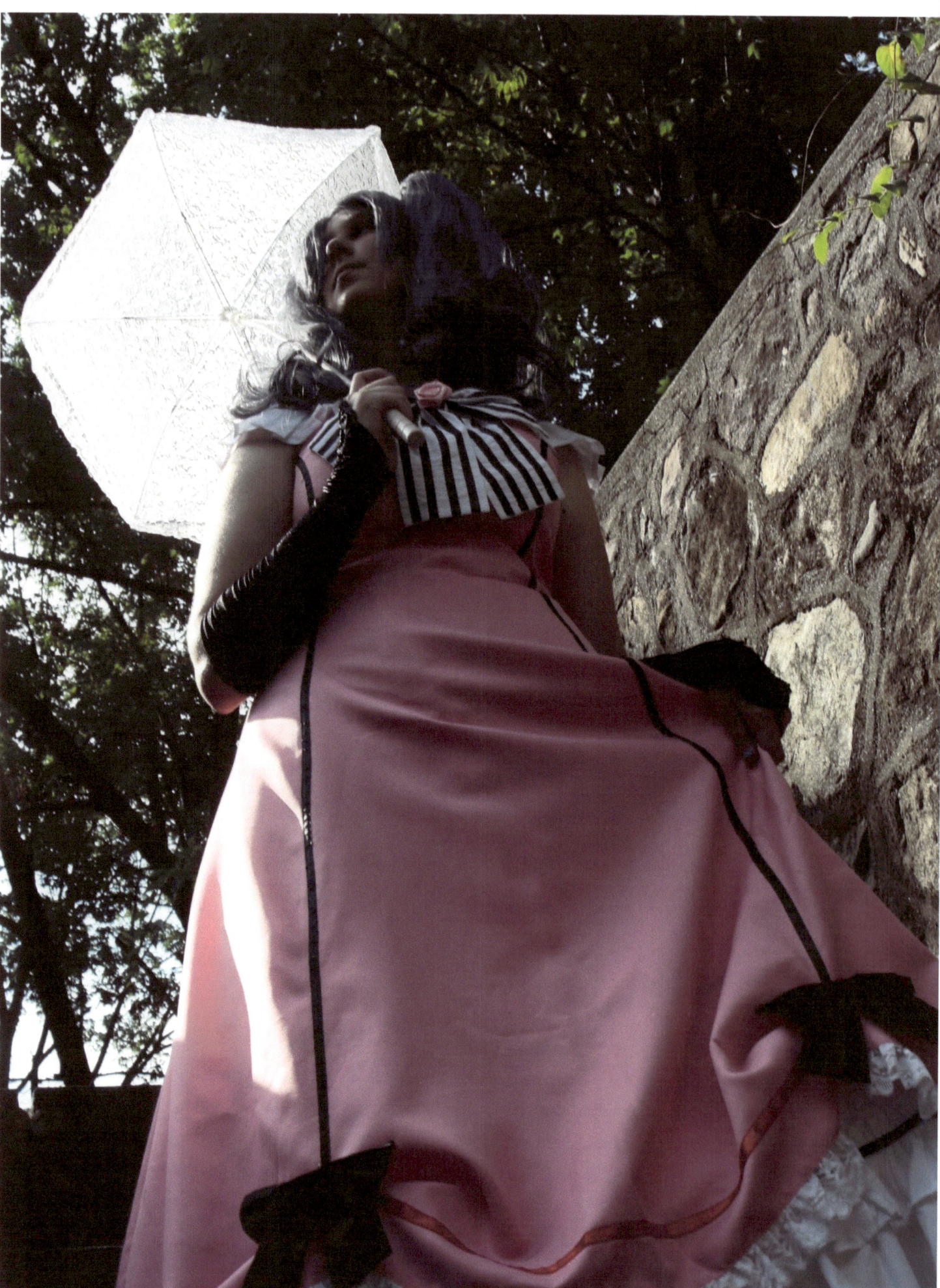

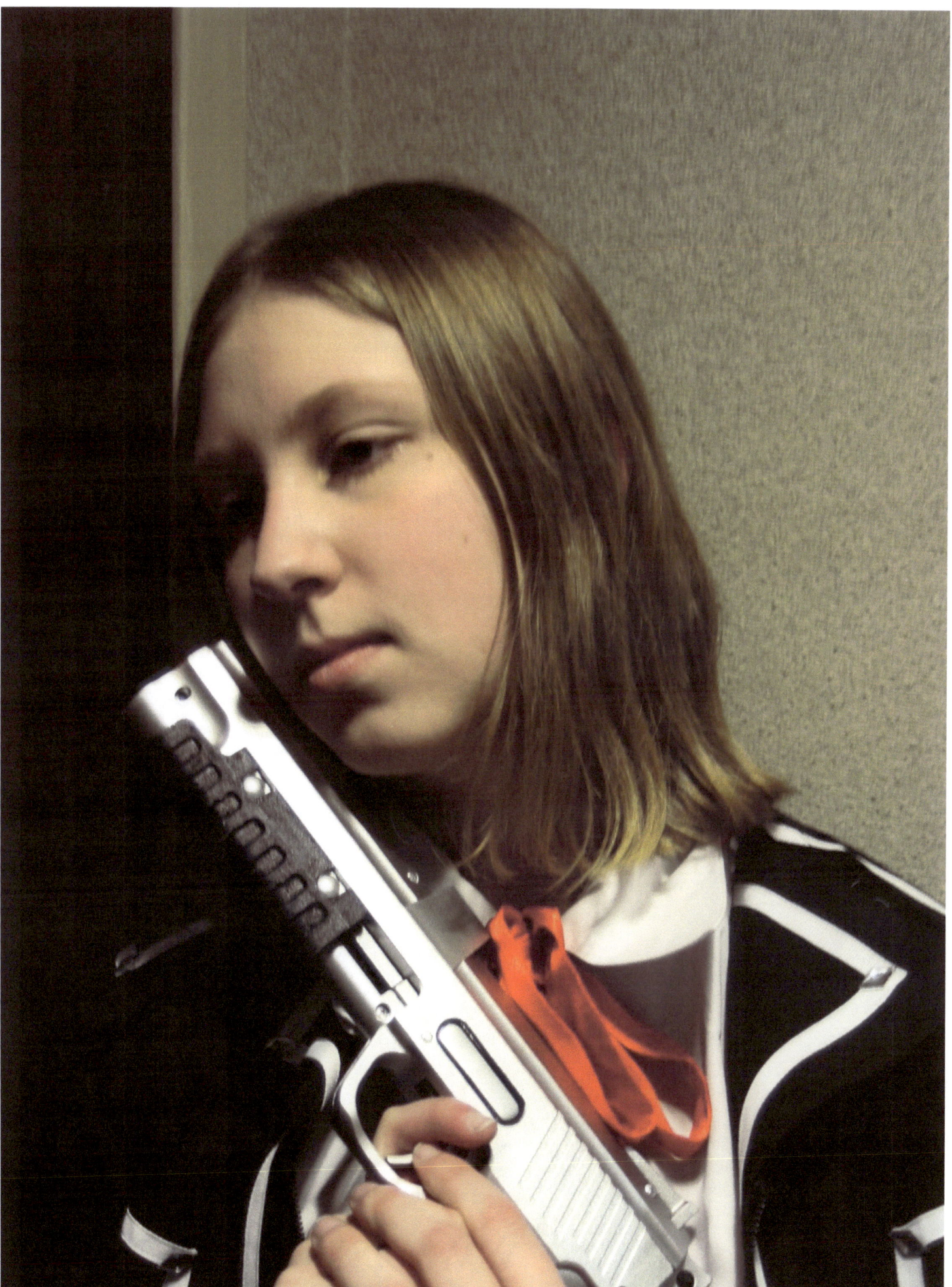

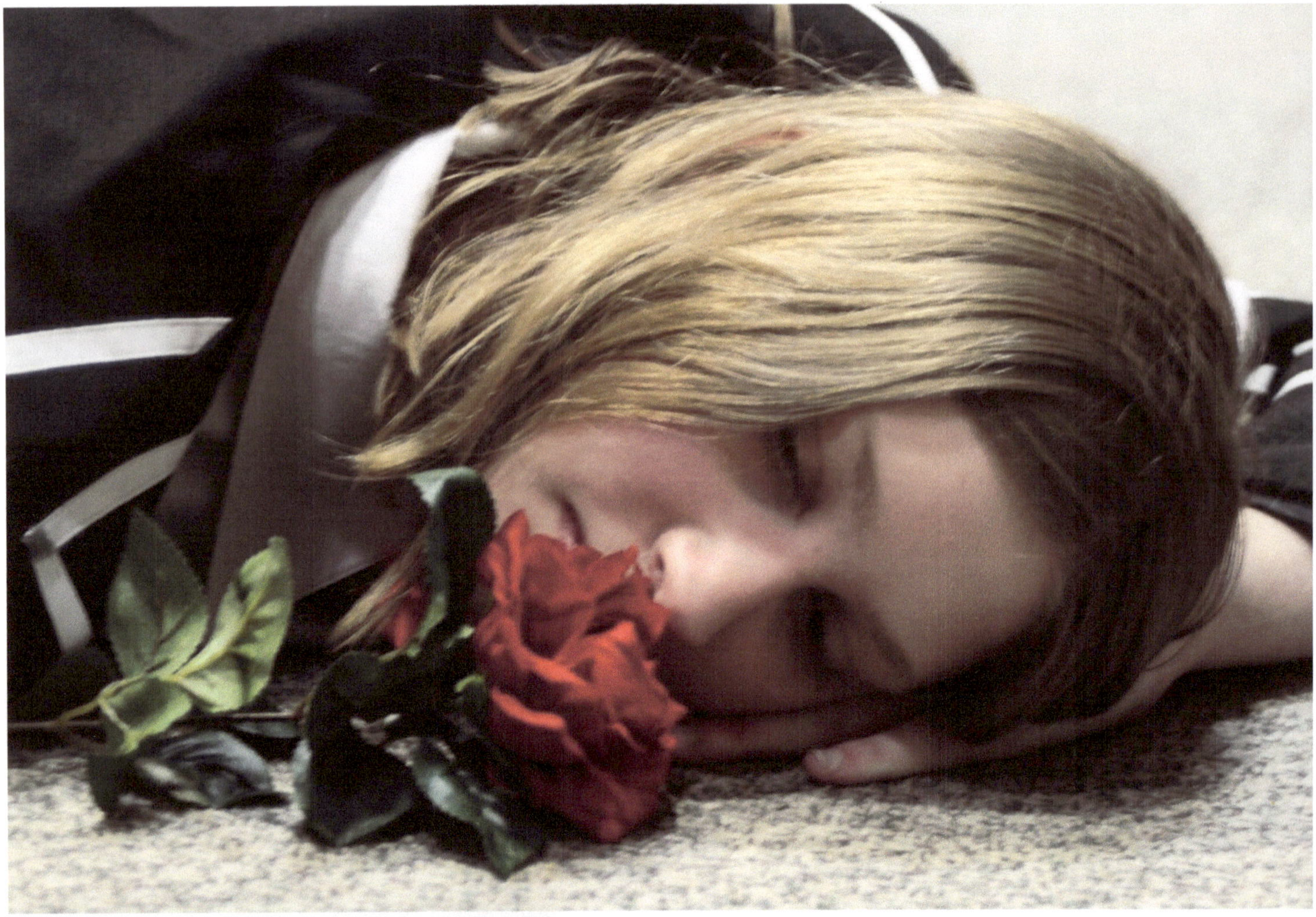

Photographer

Jason Koba has been working with mass media for over 20 years and over 1000 productions and projects, with a long resume in the entertainment and art industry.

In 1996 he created StoryStick Productions which gave an outlet for his projects to build and grow into their own. Together with his fans, friends, and family he hopes to bring a new look to his visions of life and art.

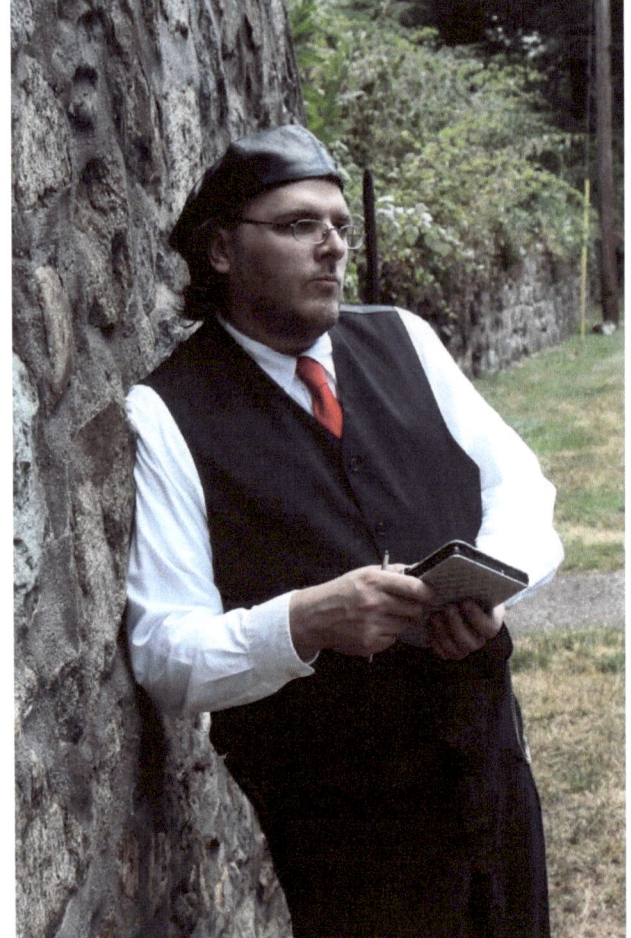

www.storystick.com

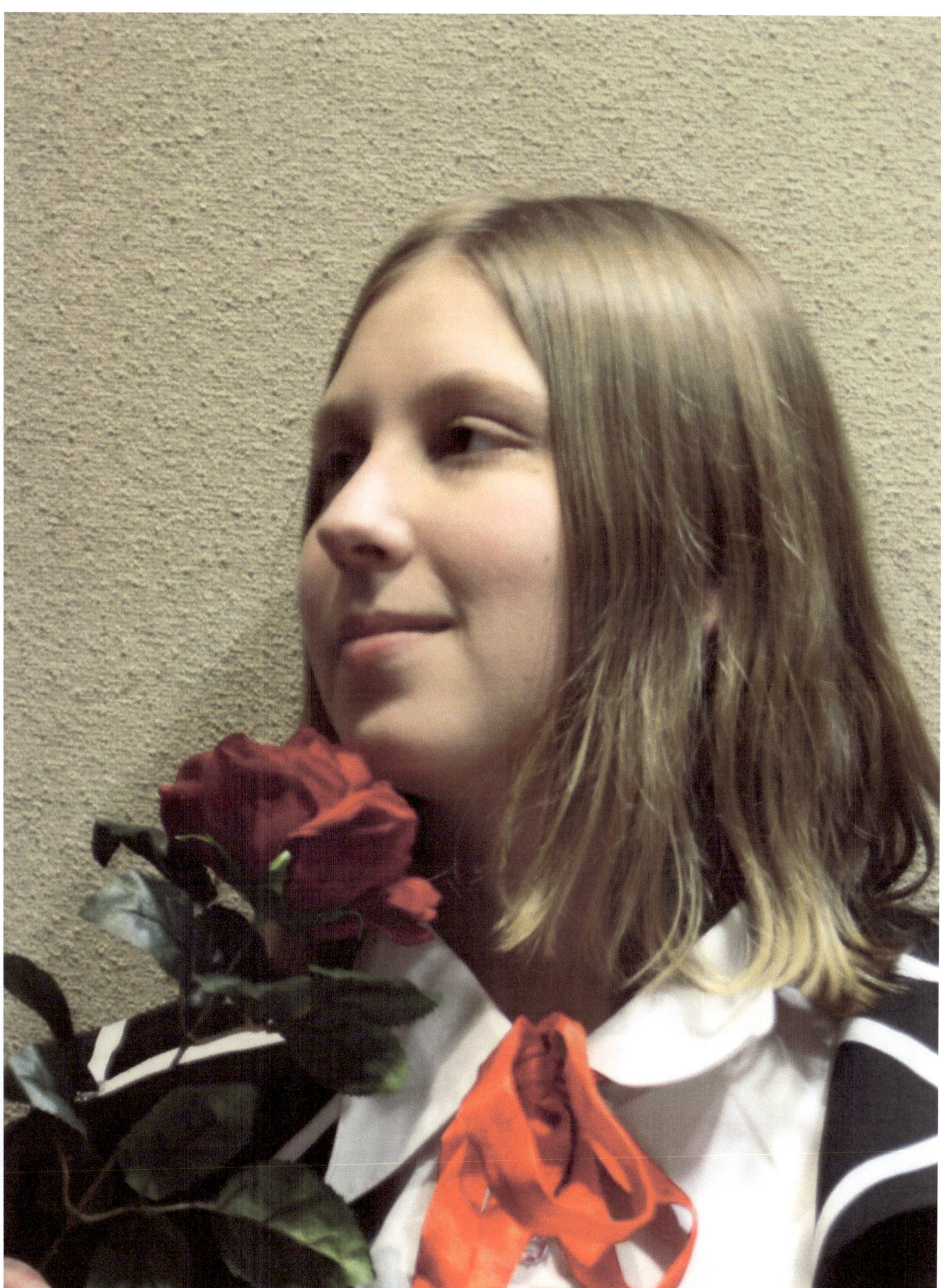

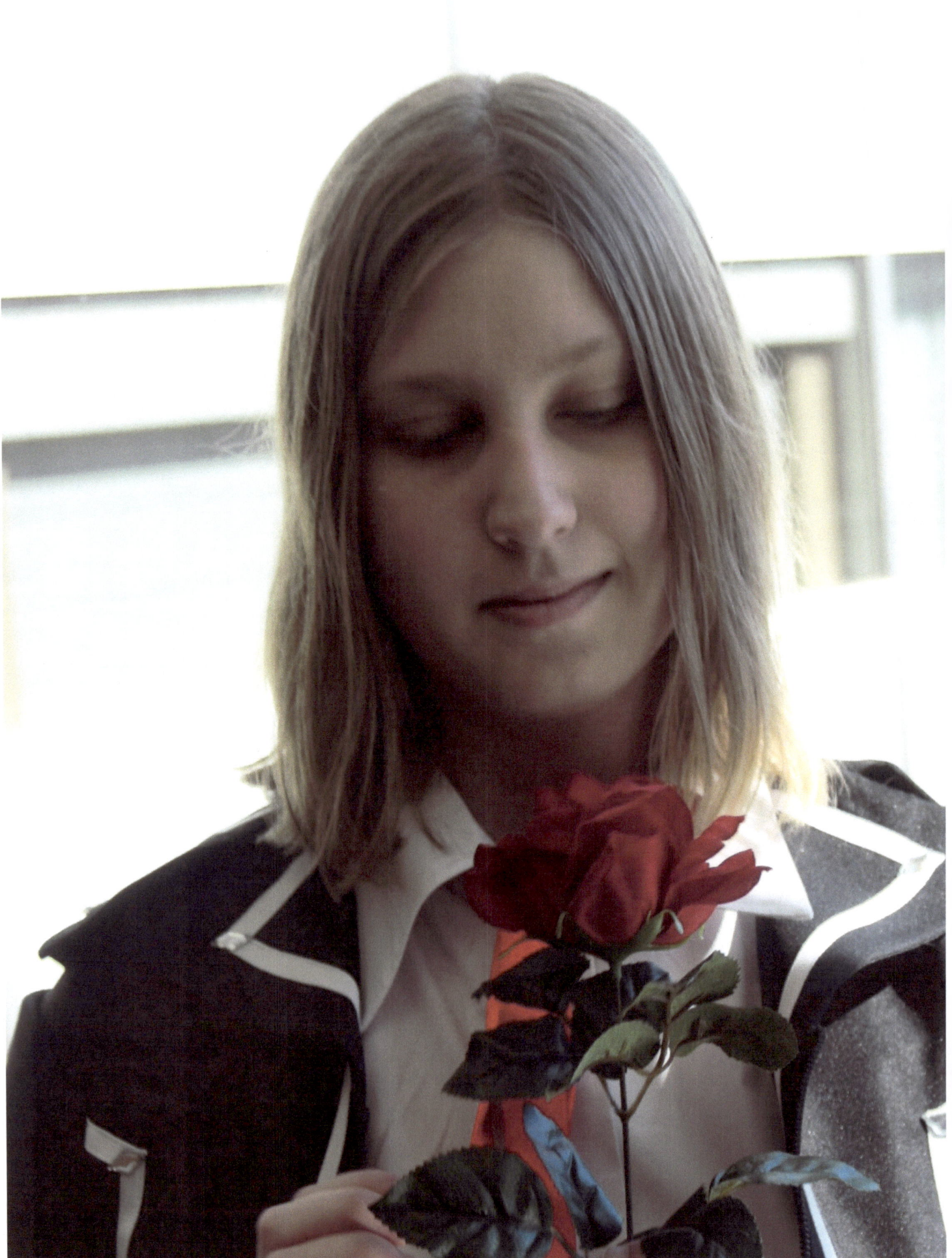

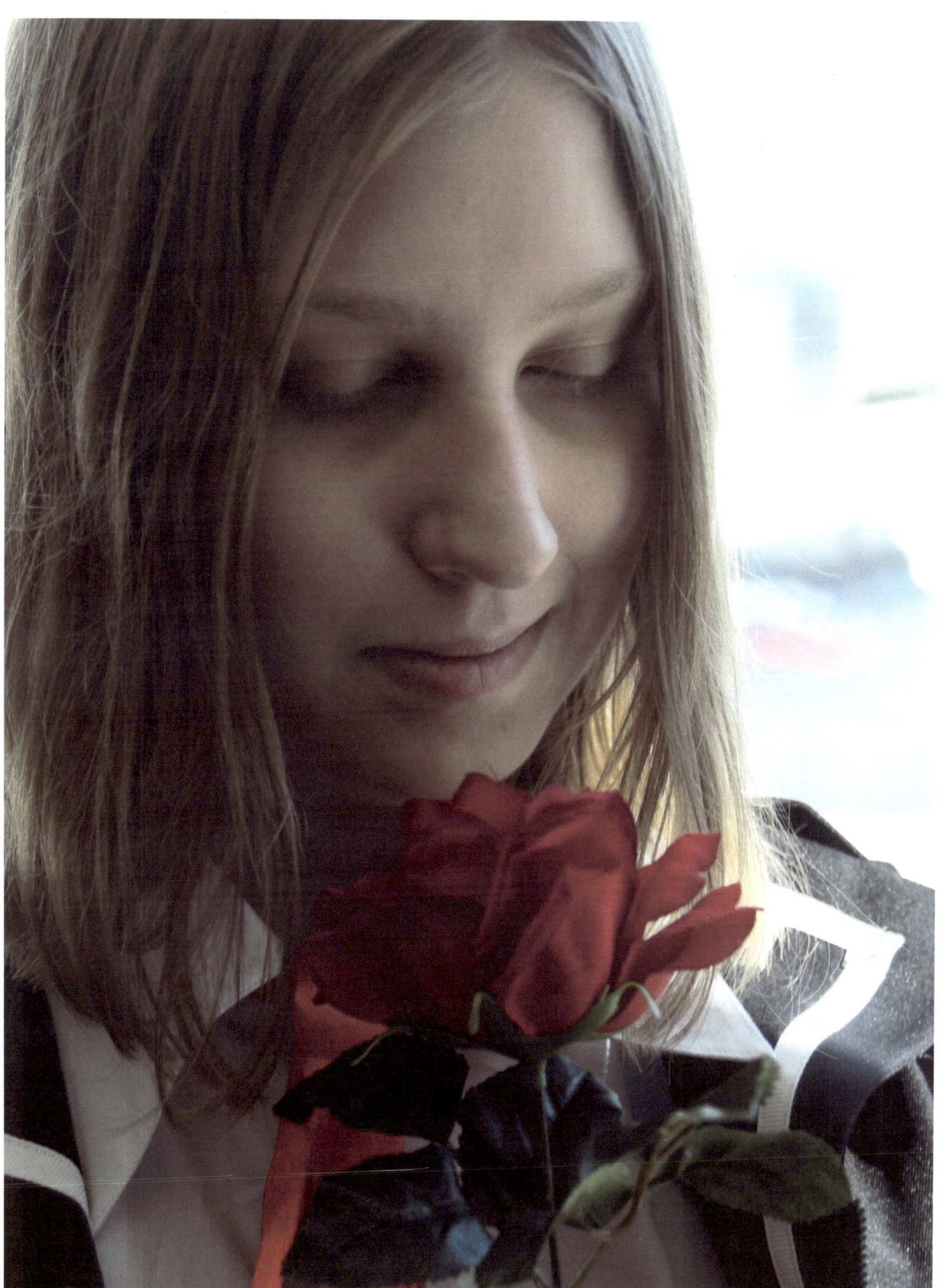

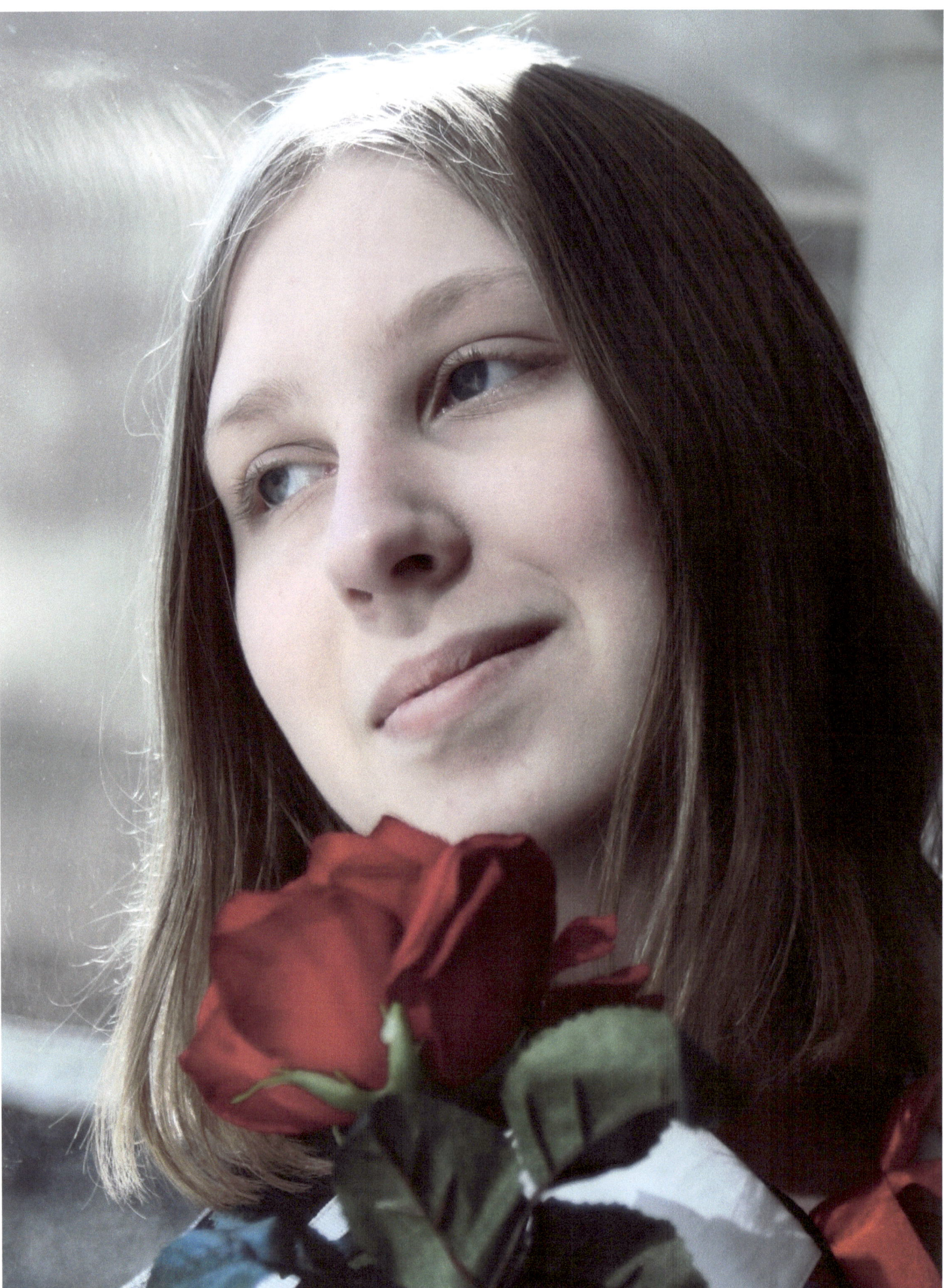

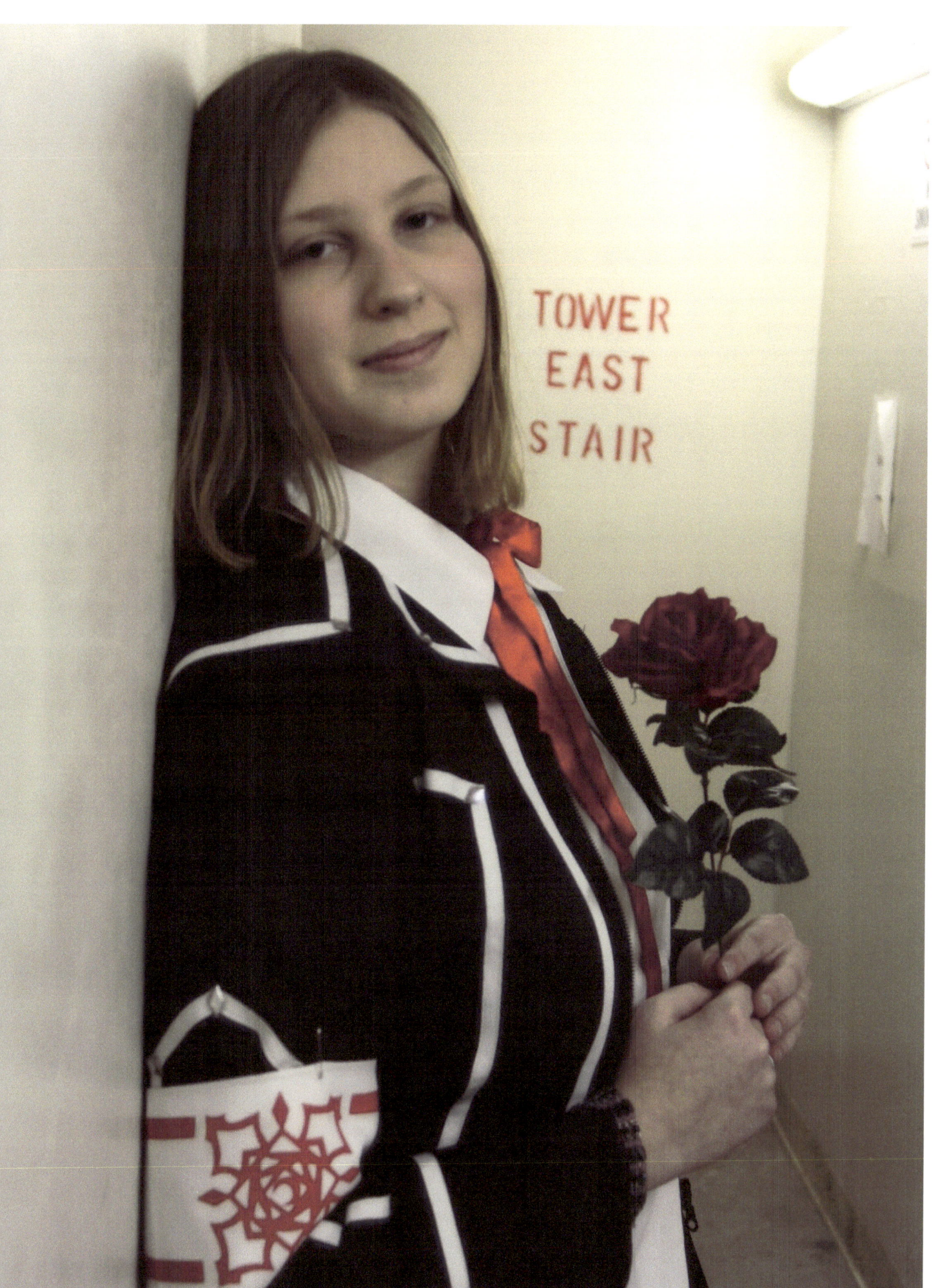

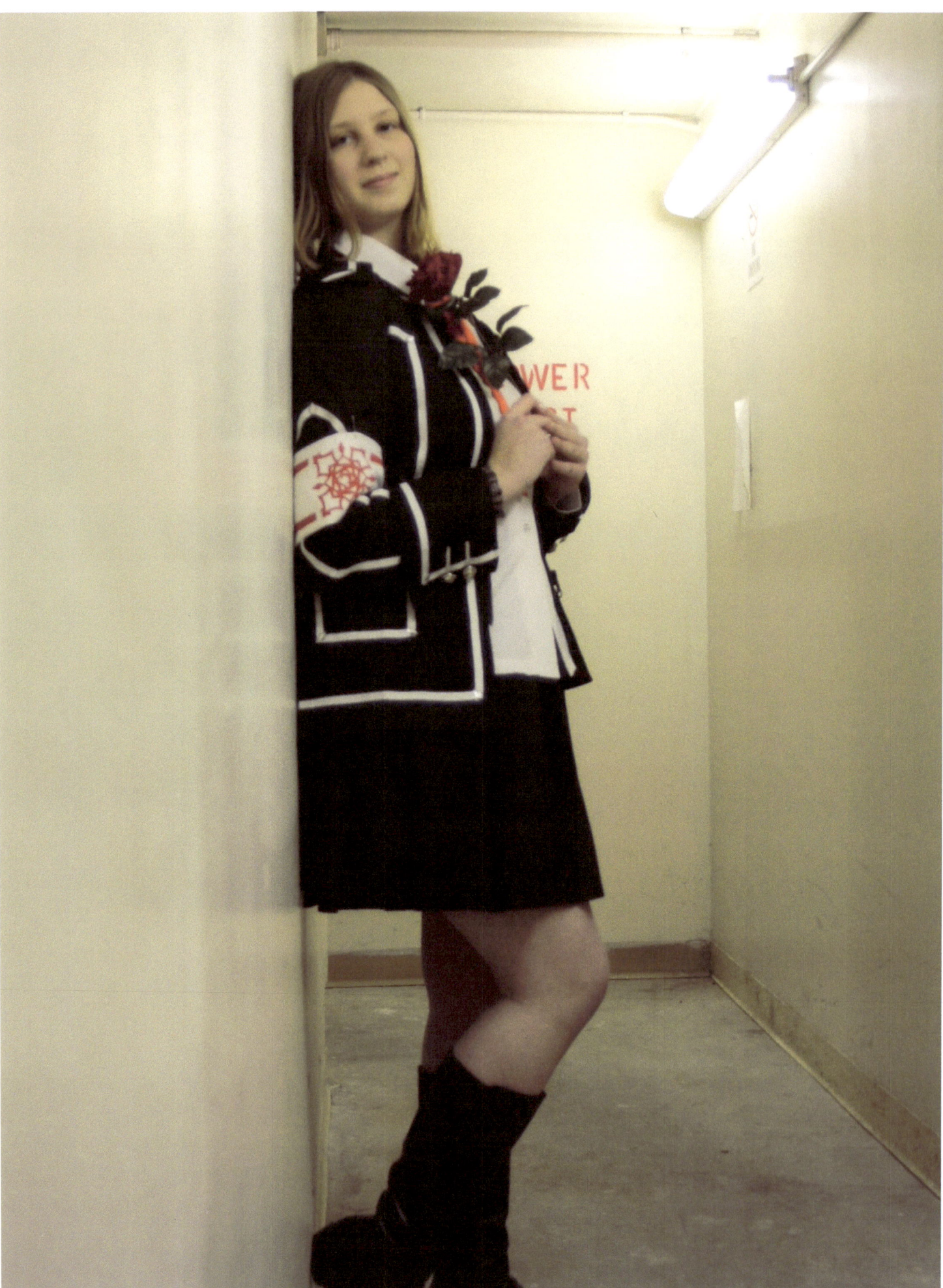

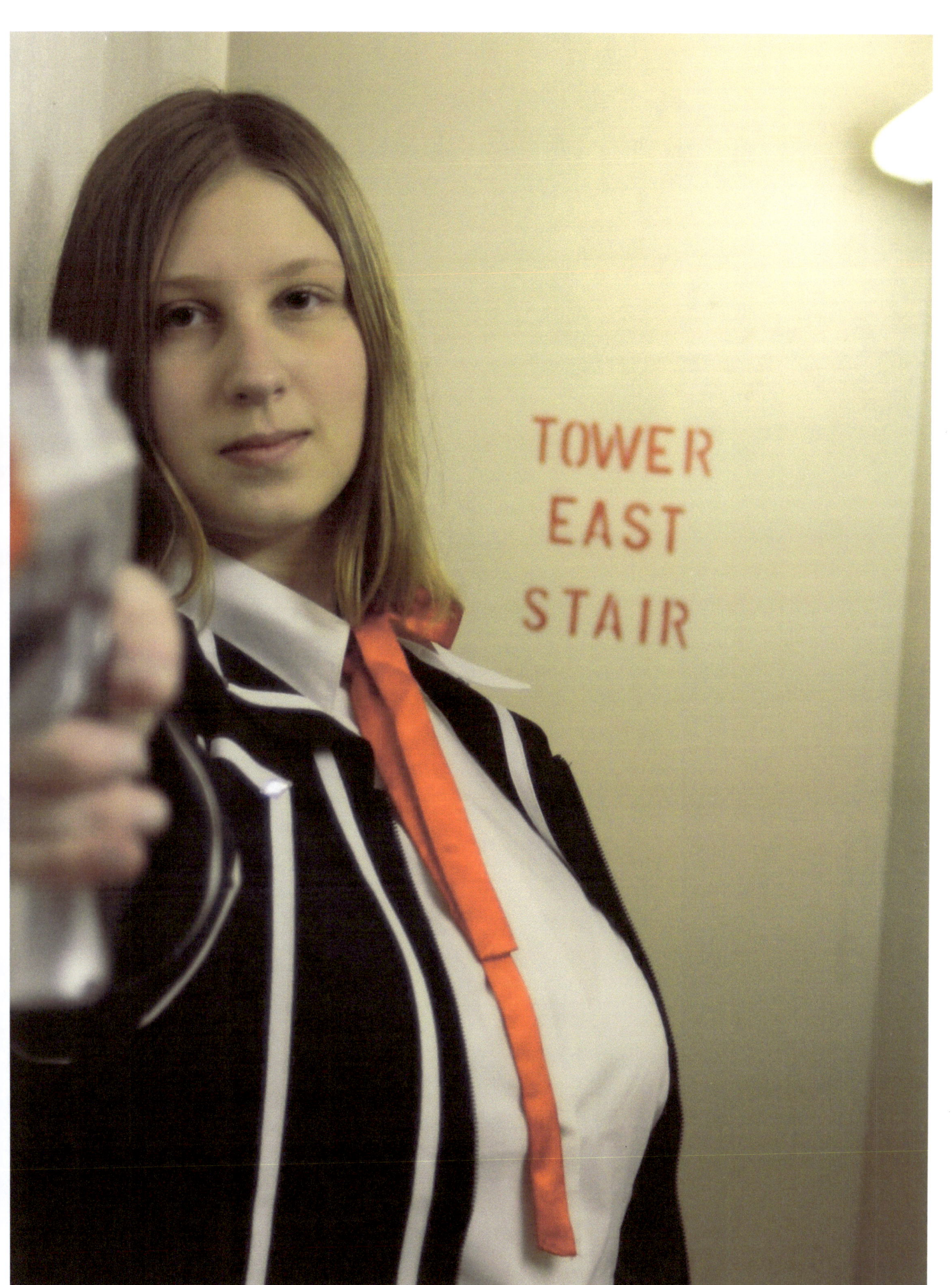

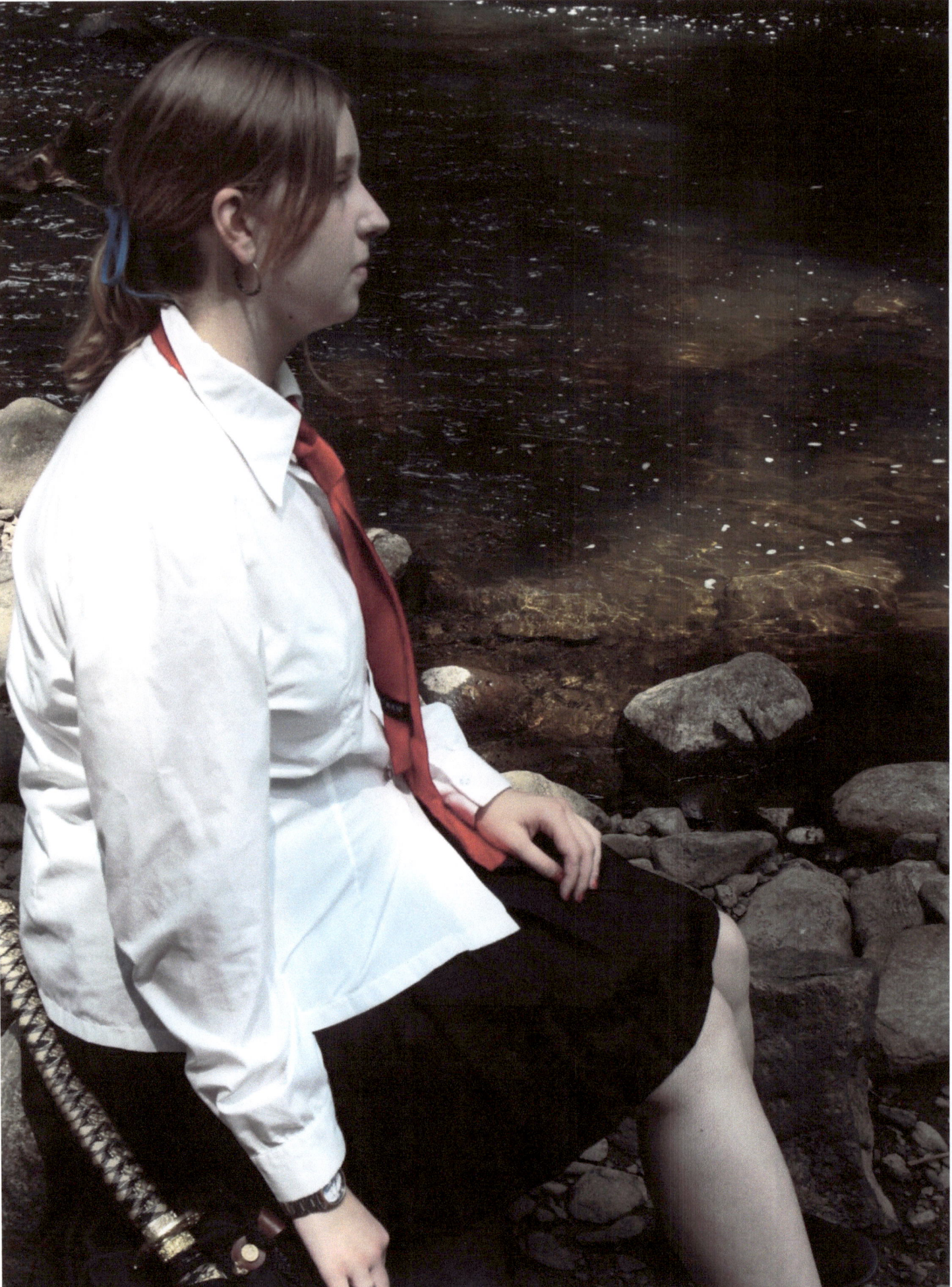

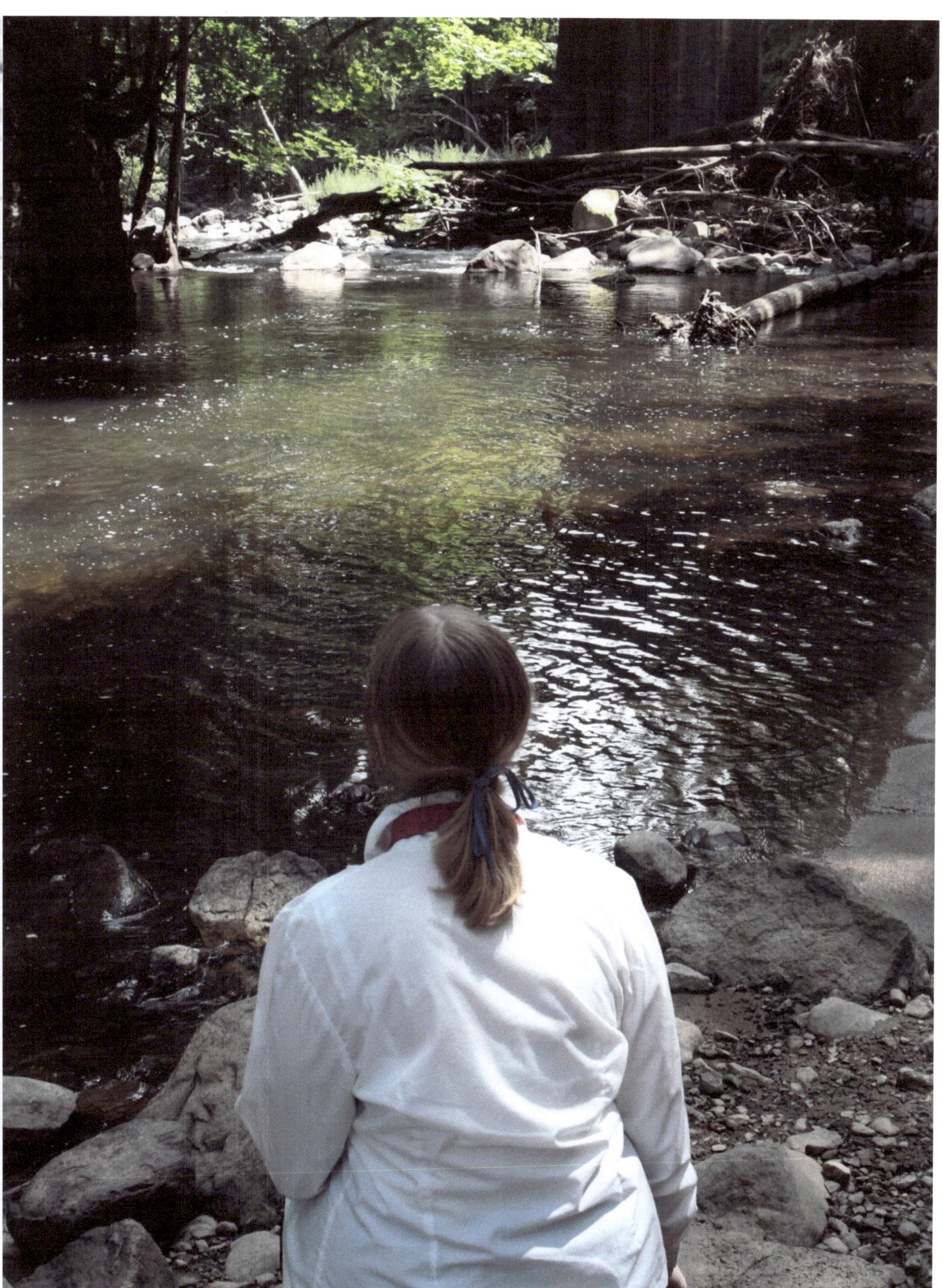

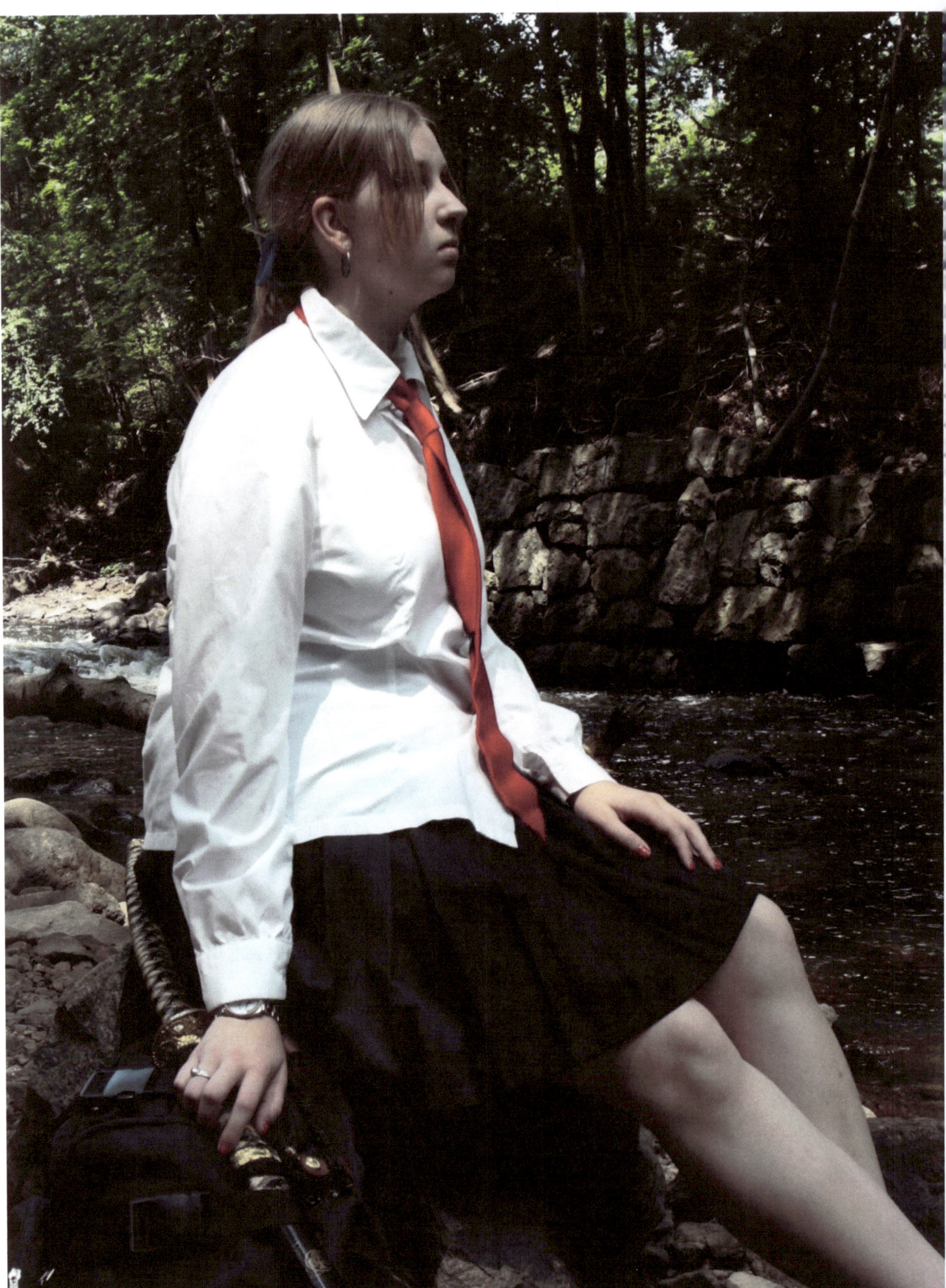

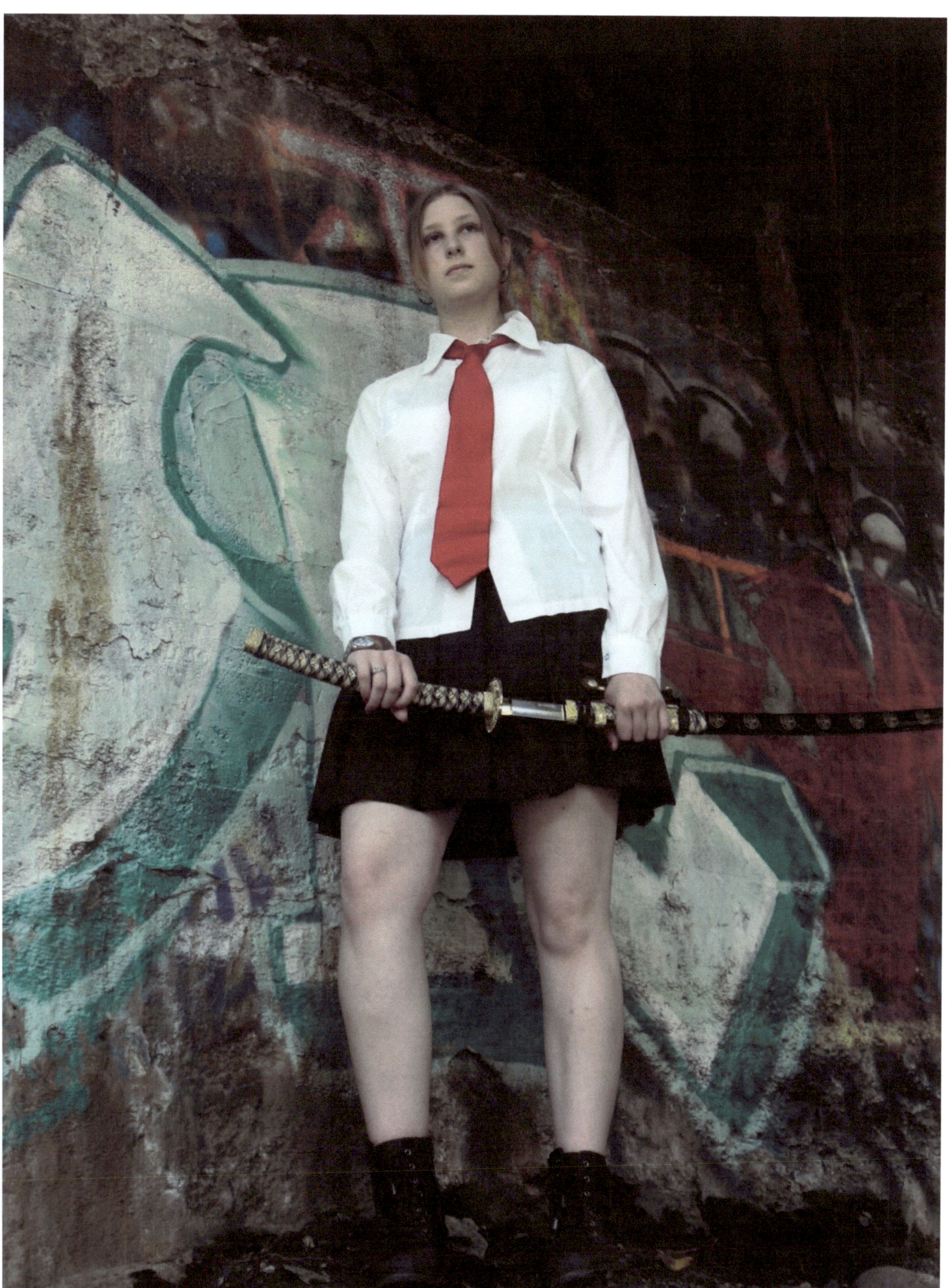

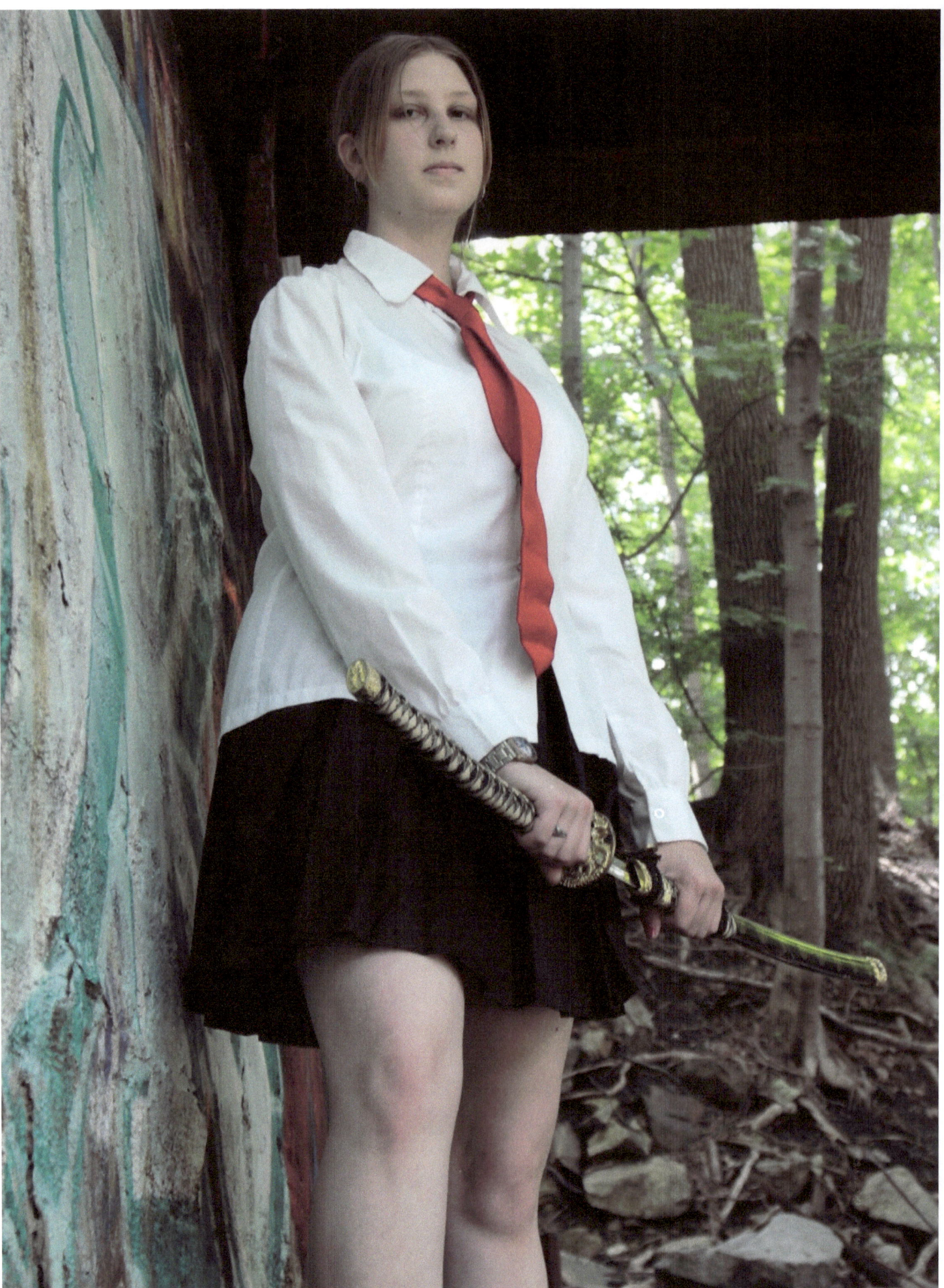

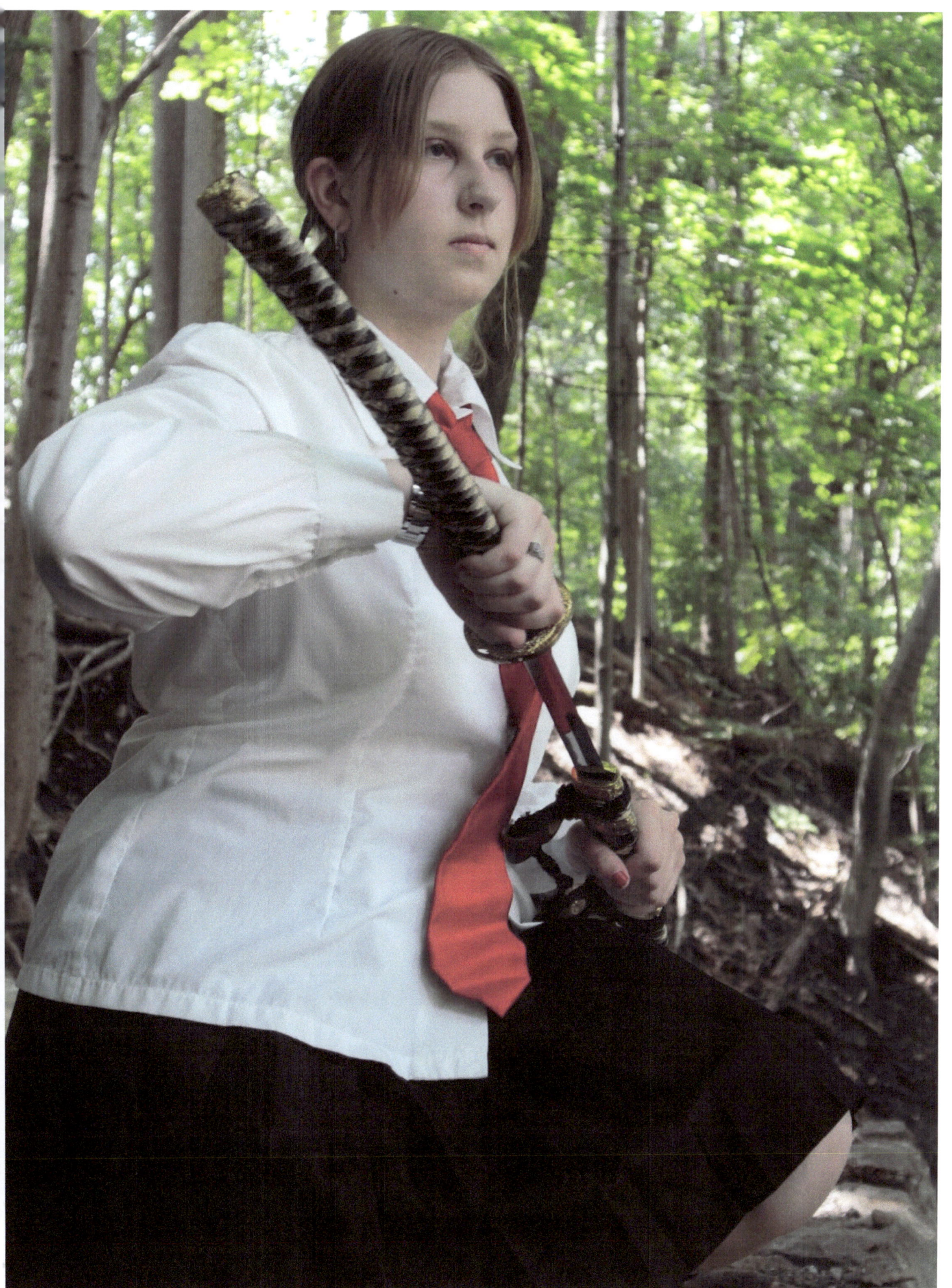

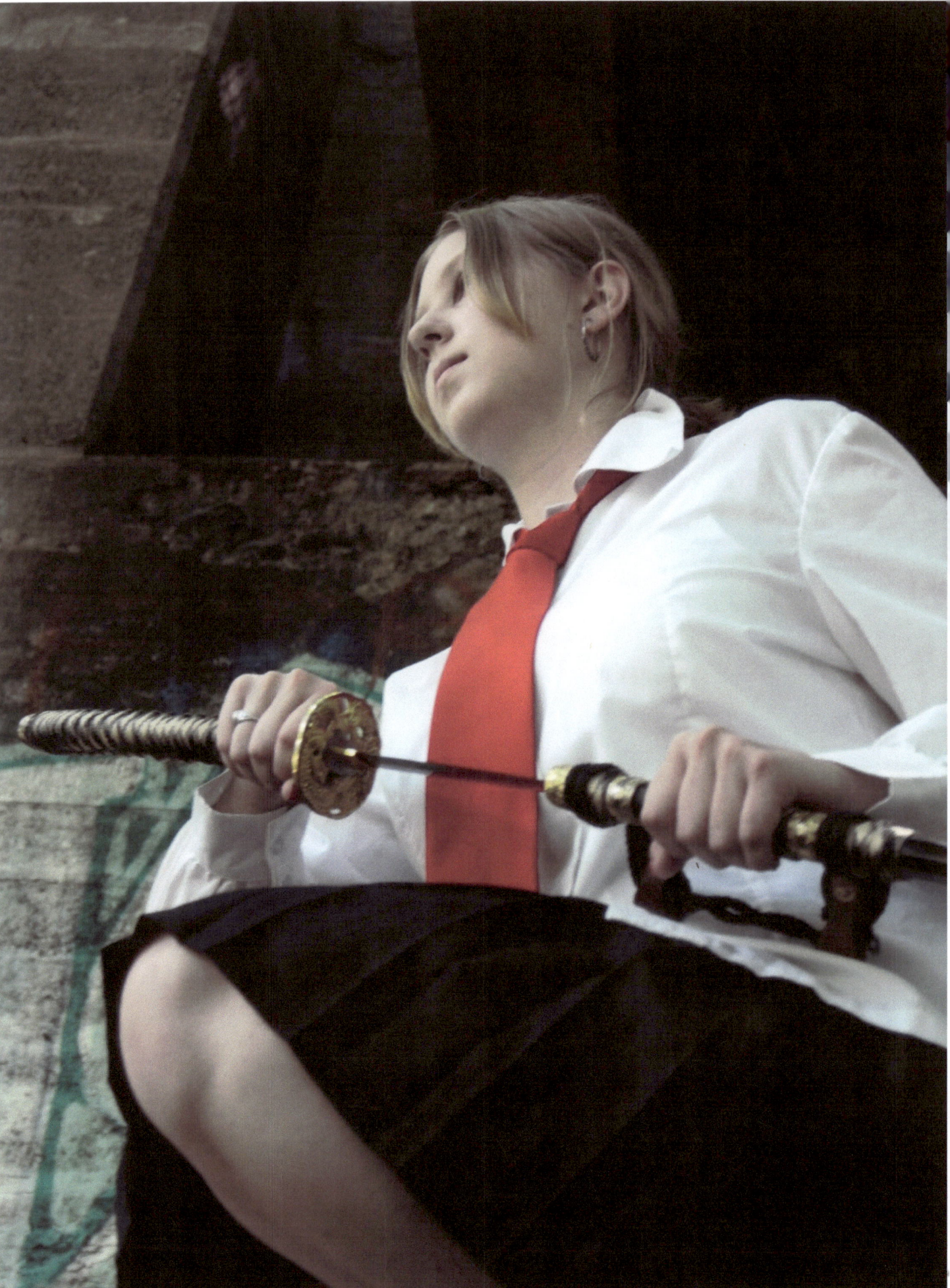

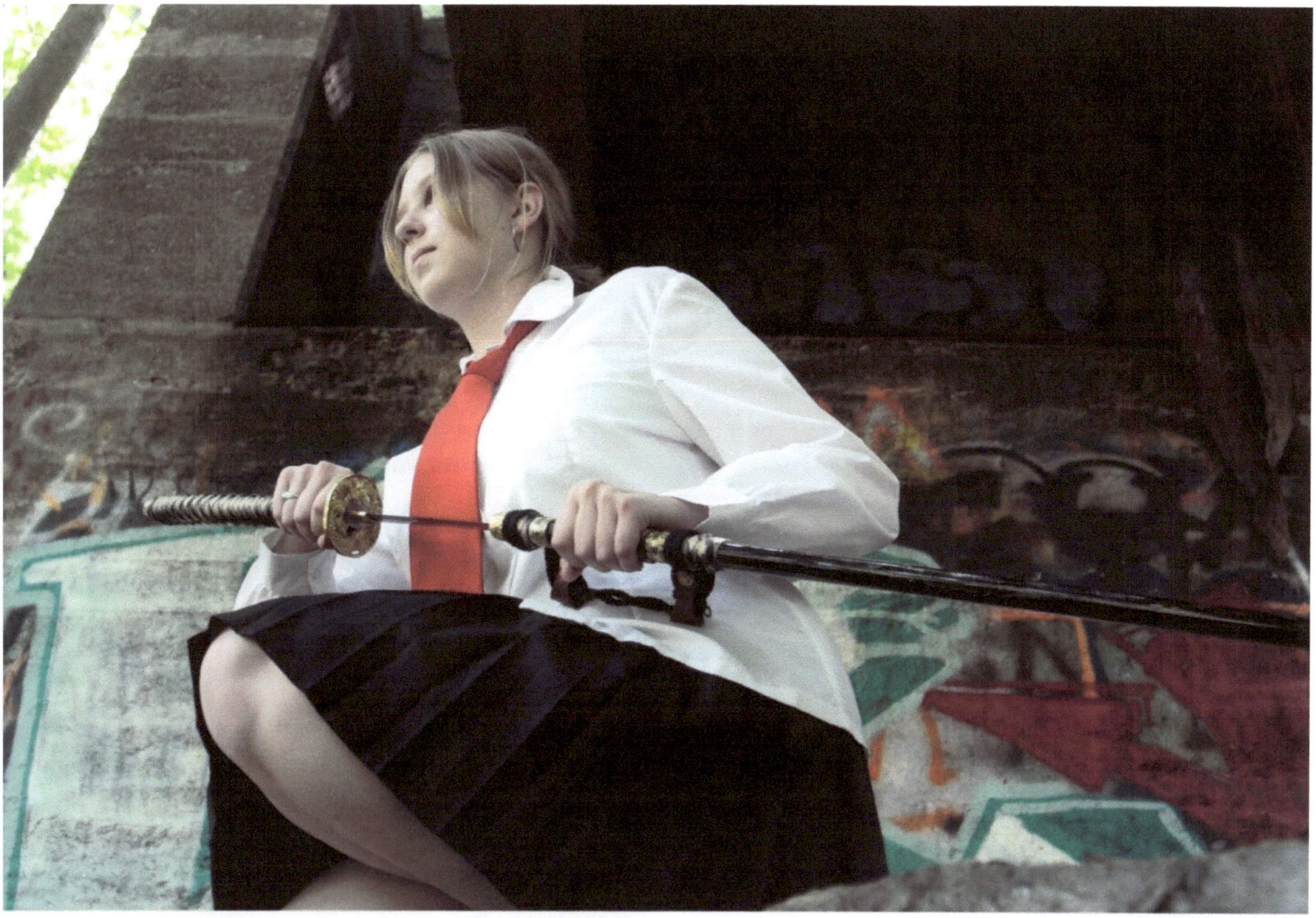

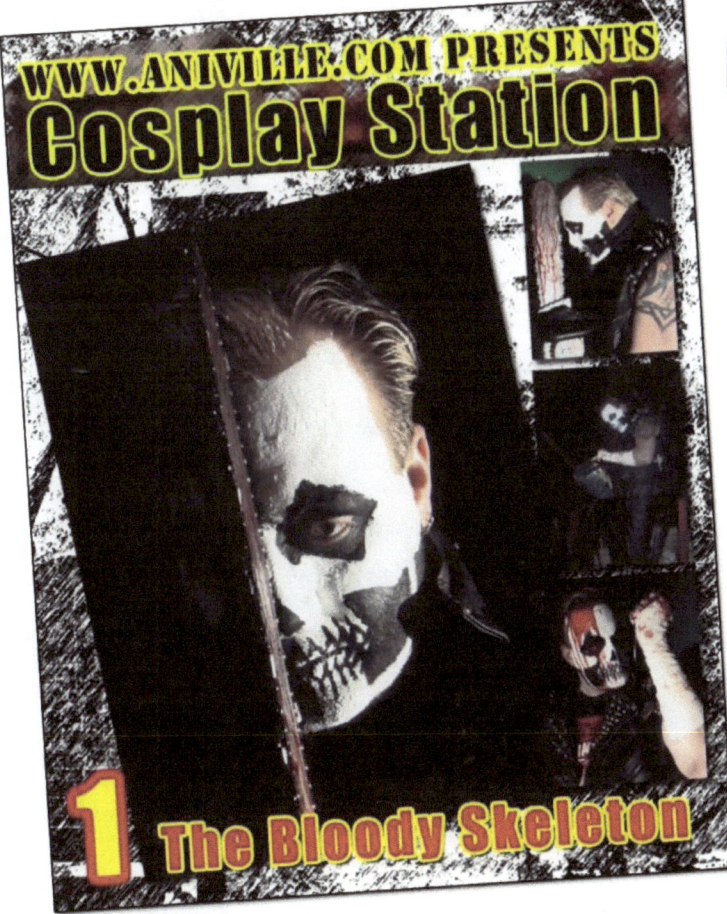

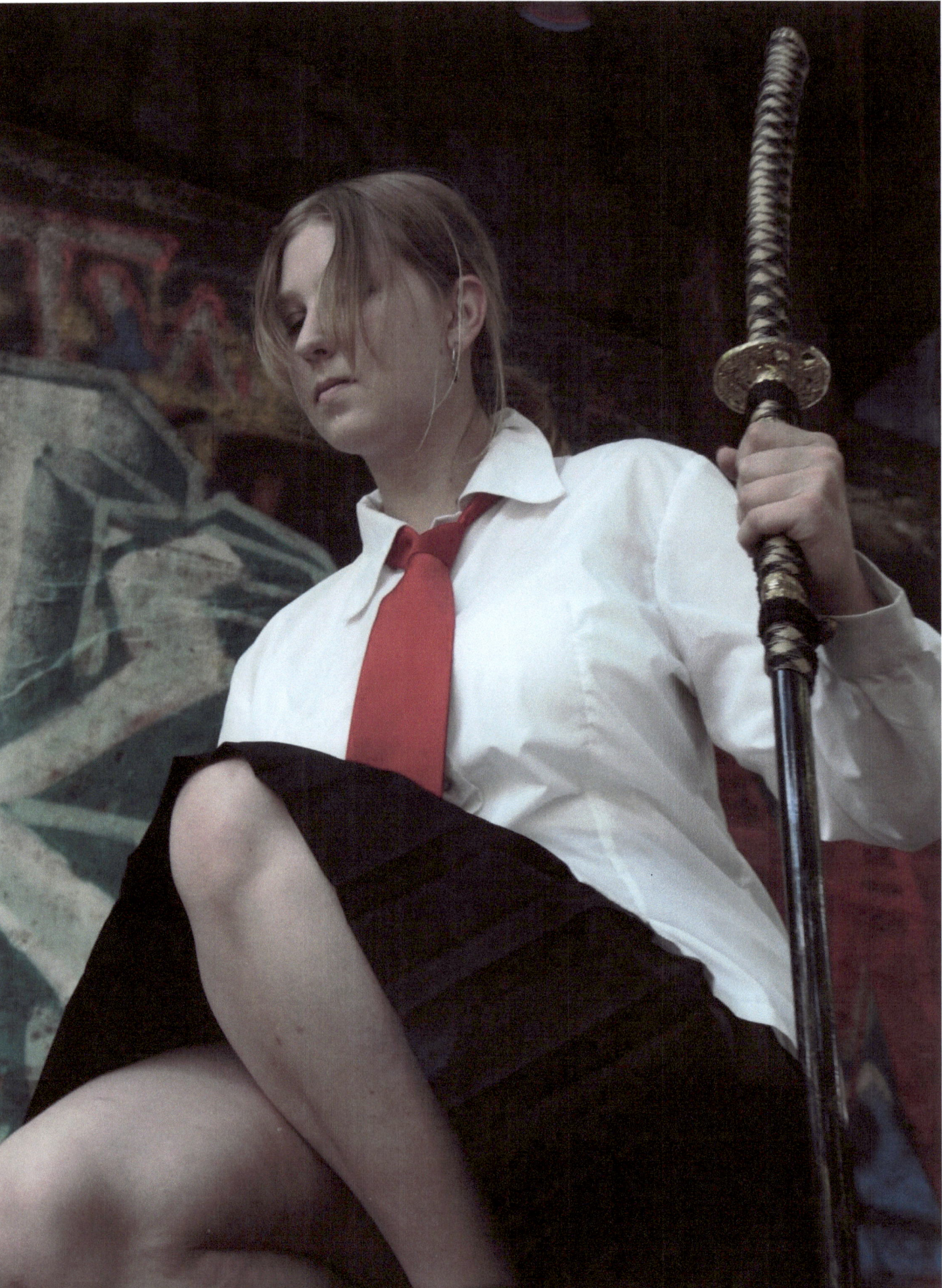

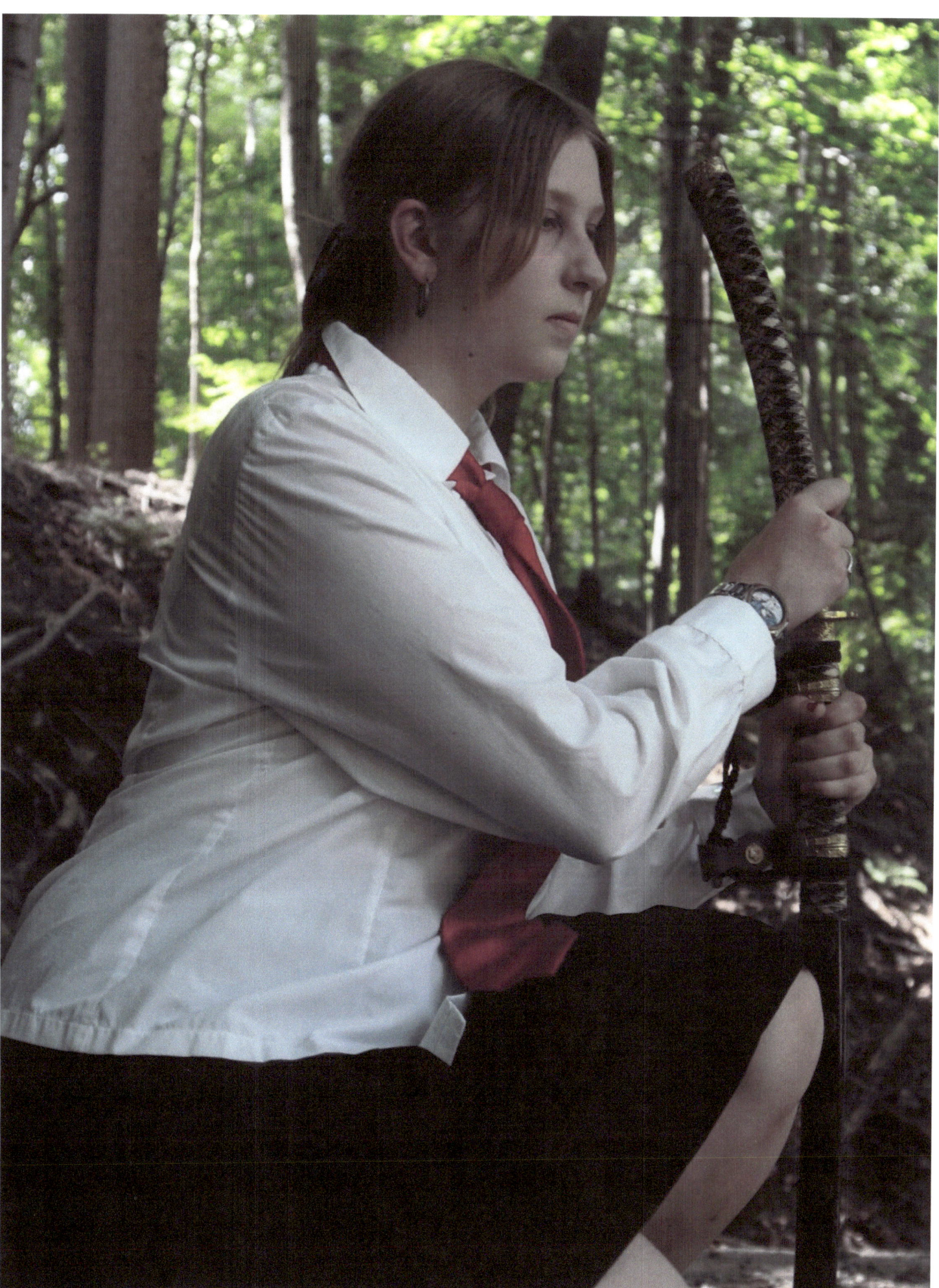

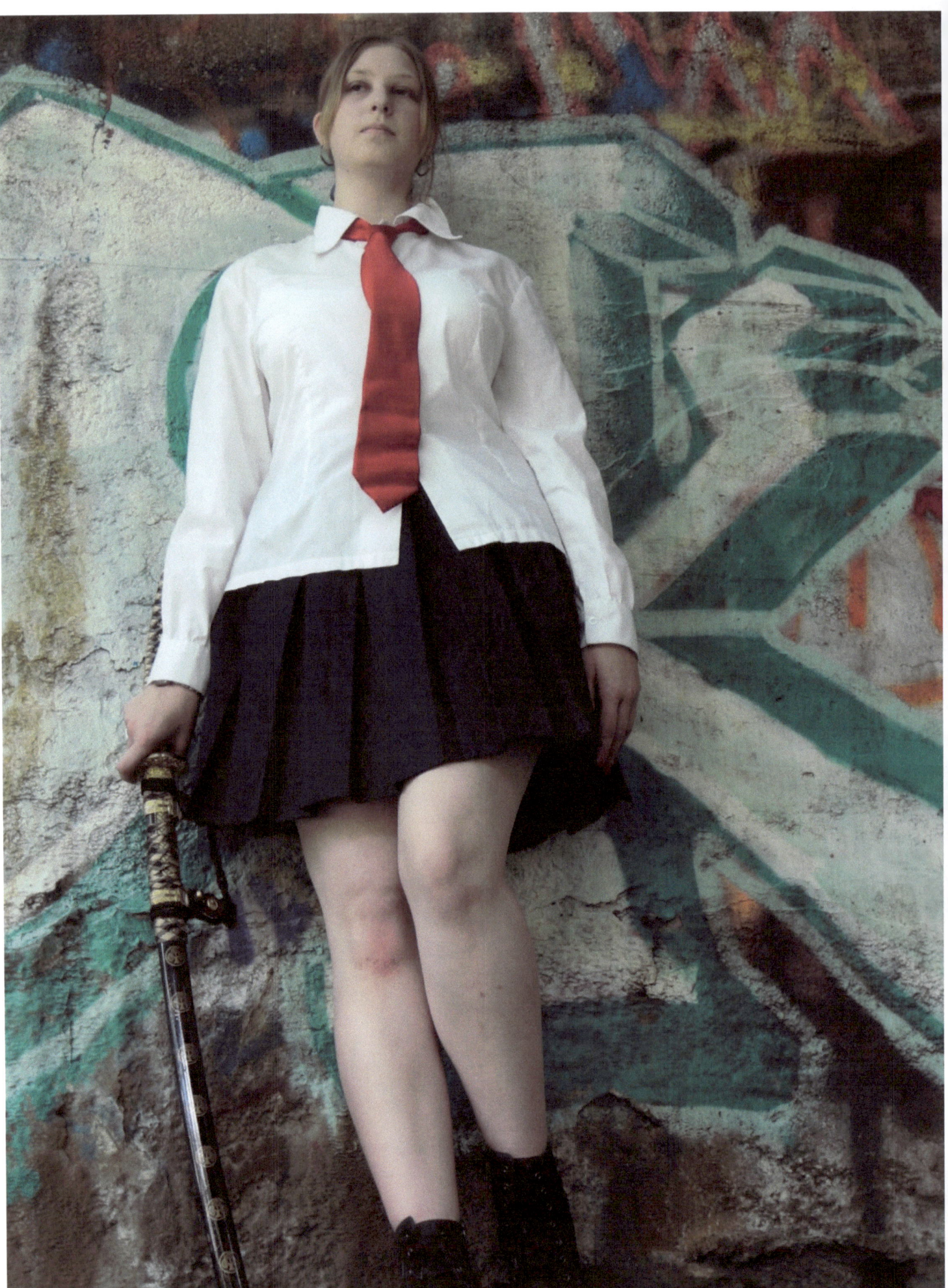

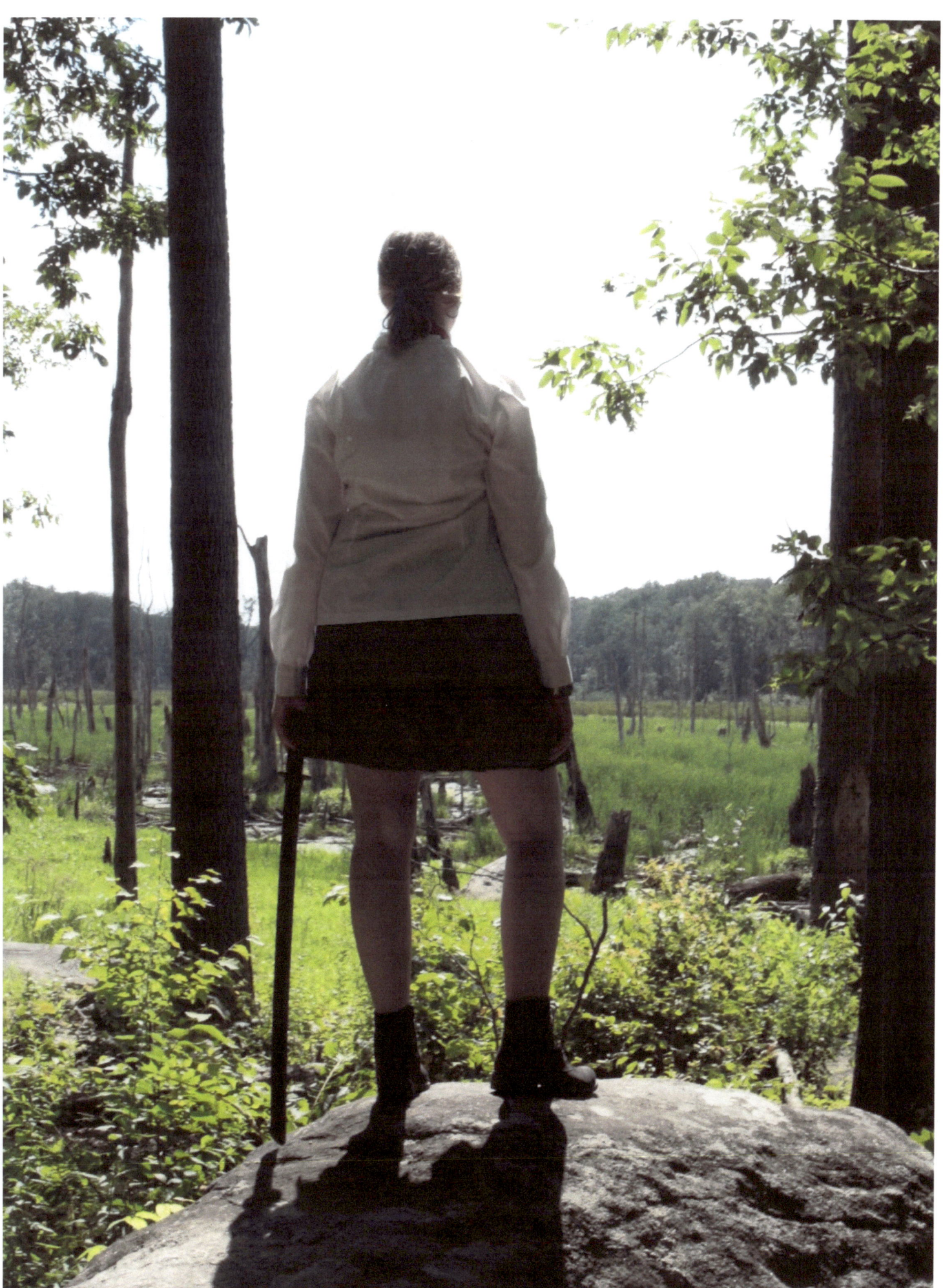

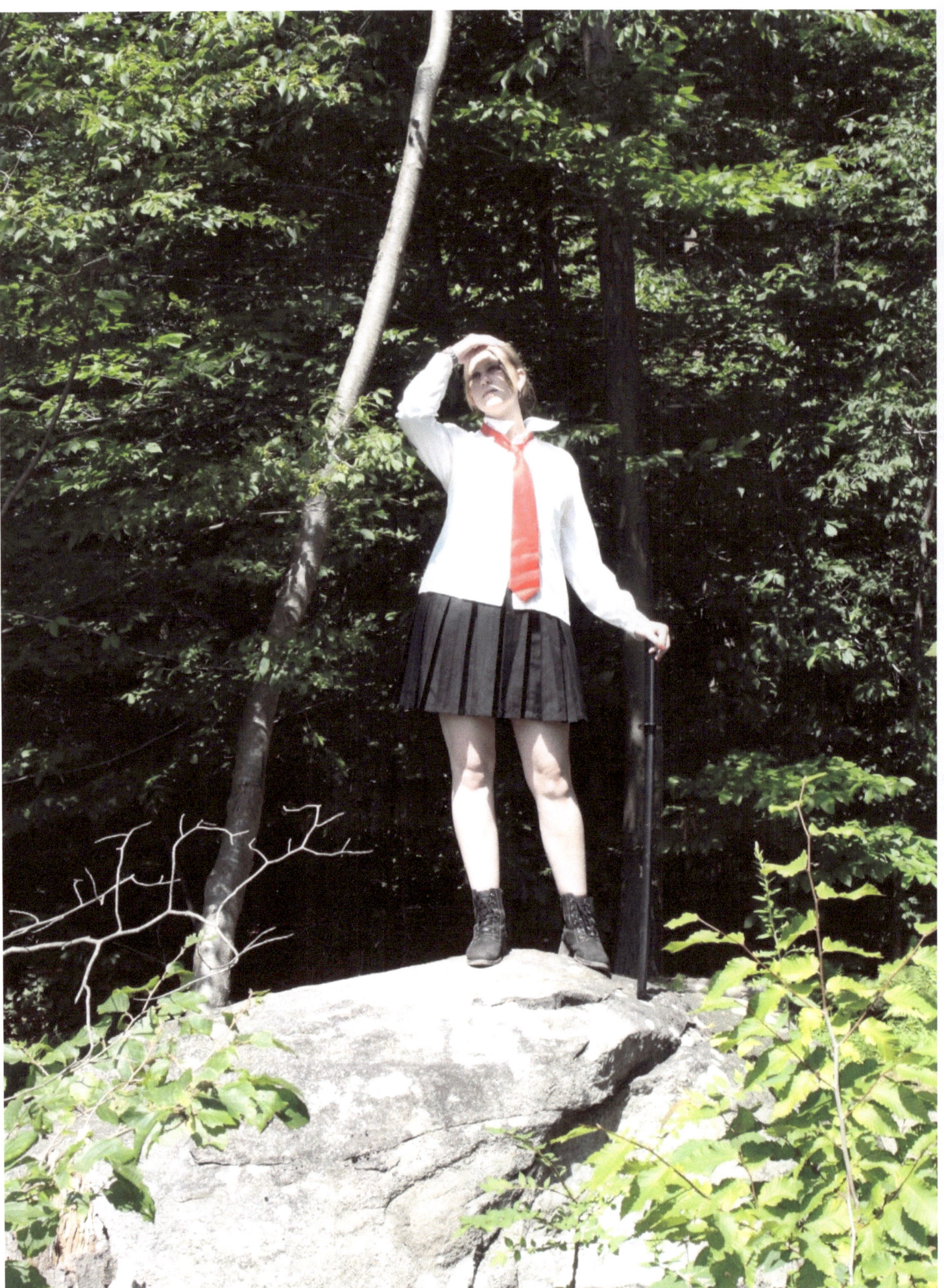

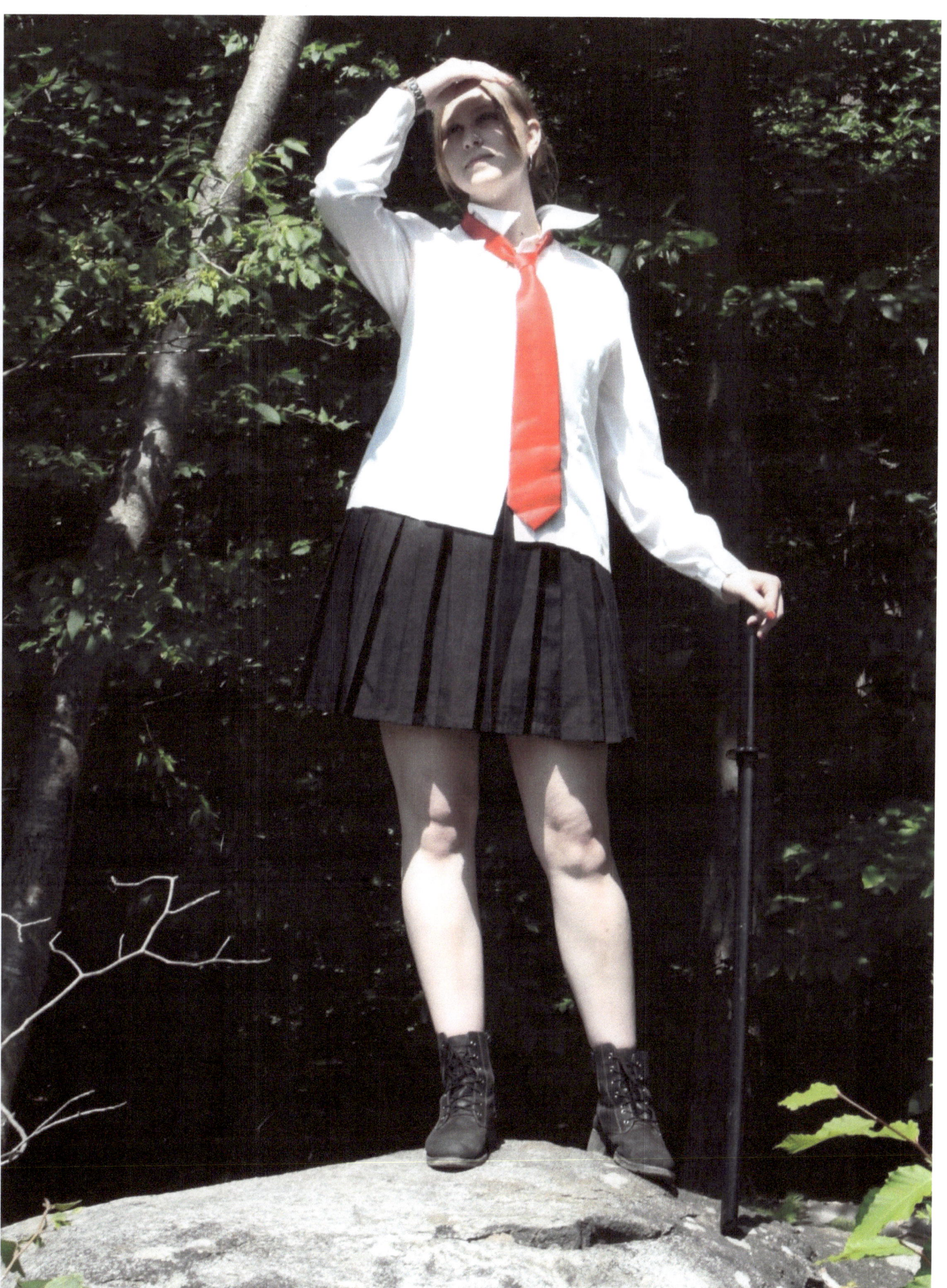

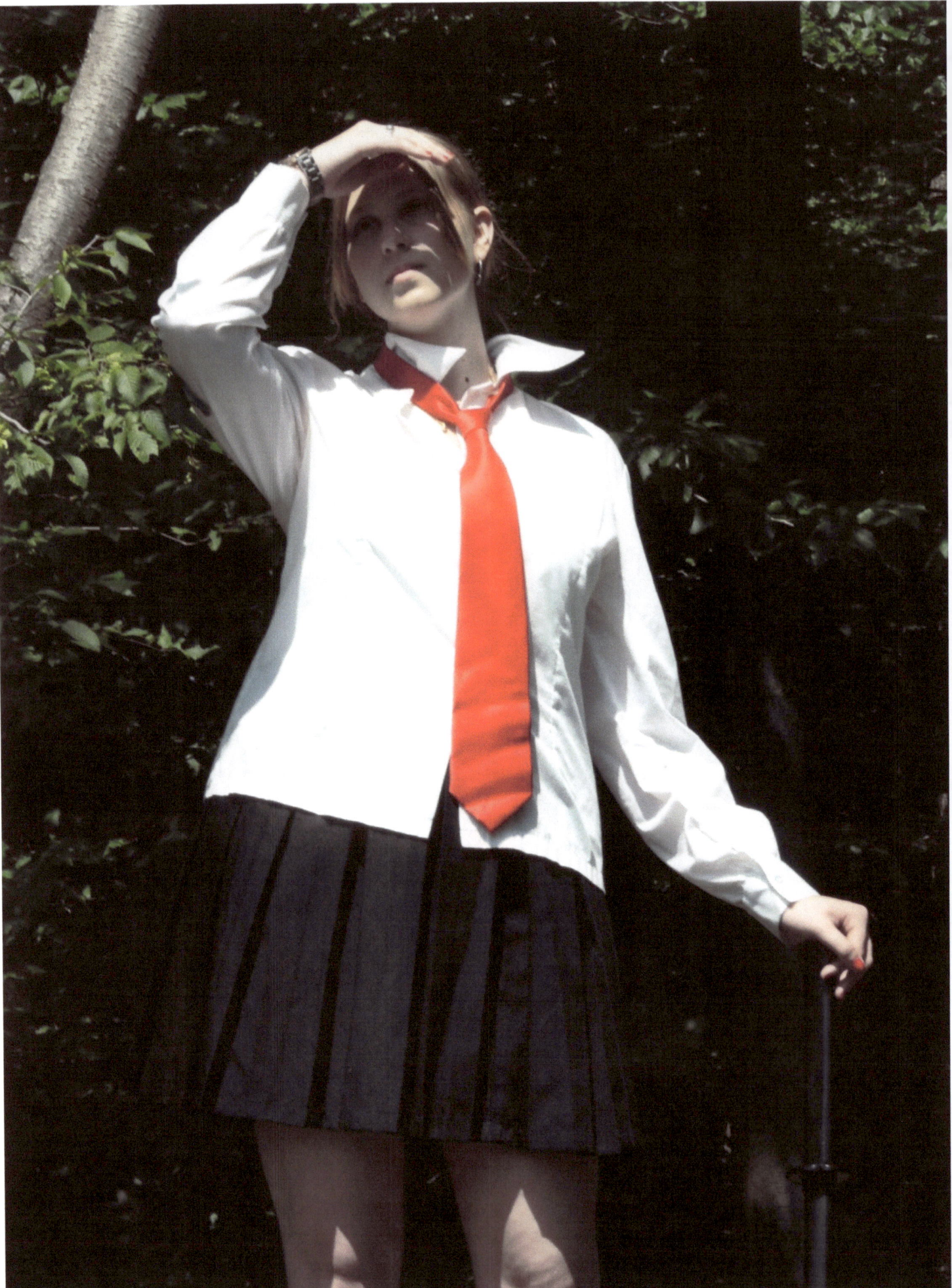

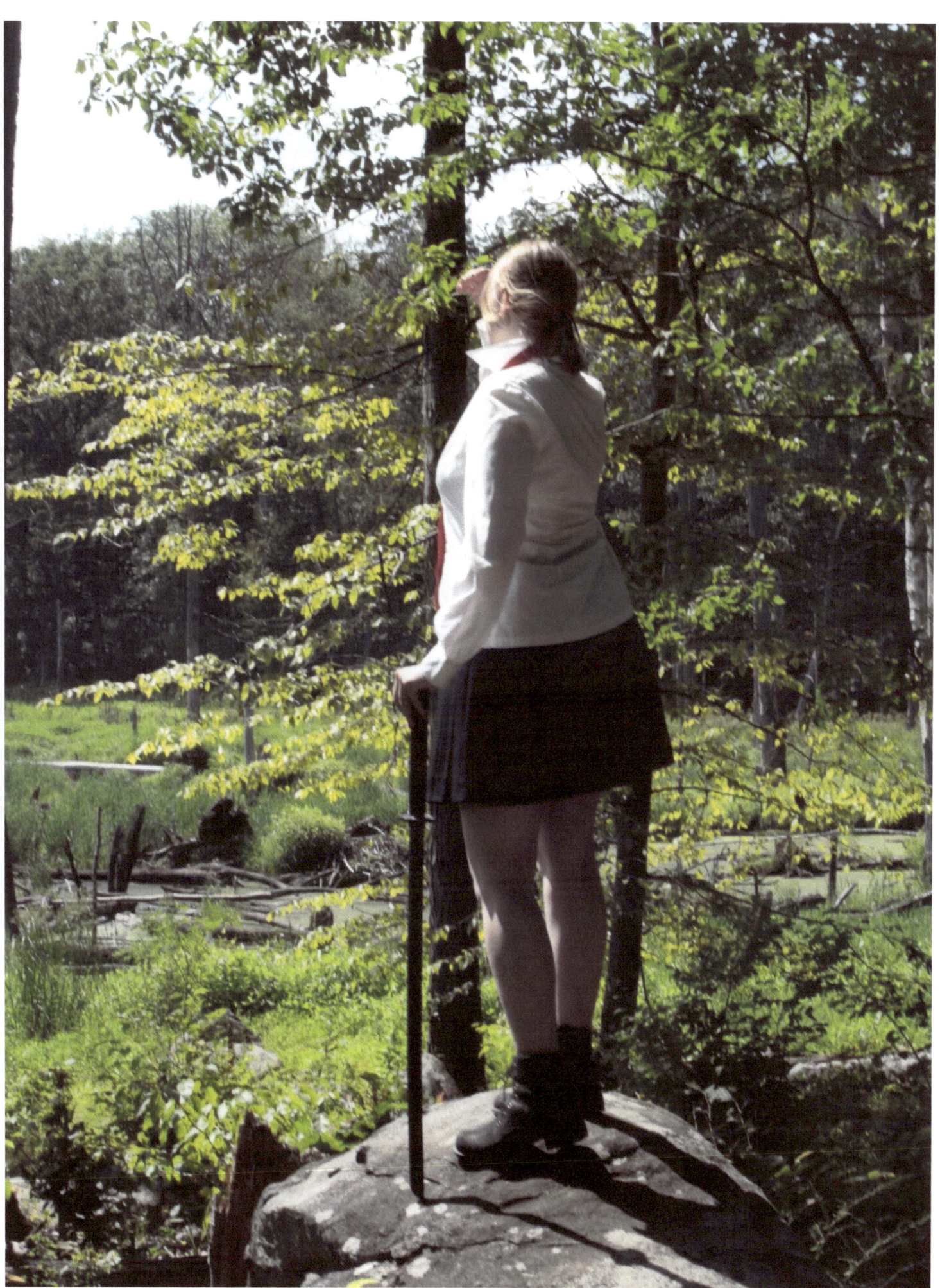

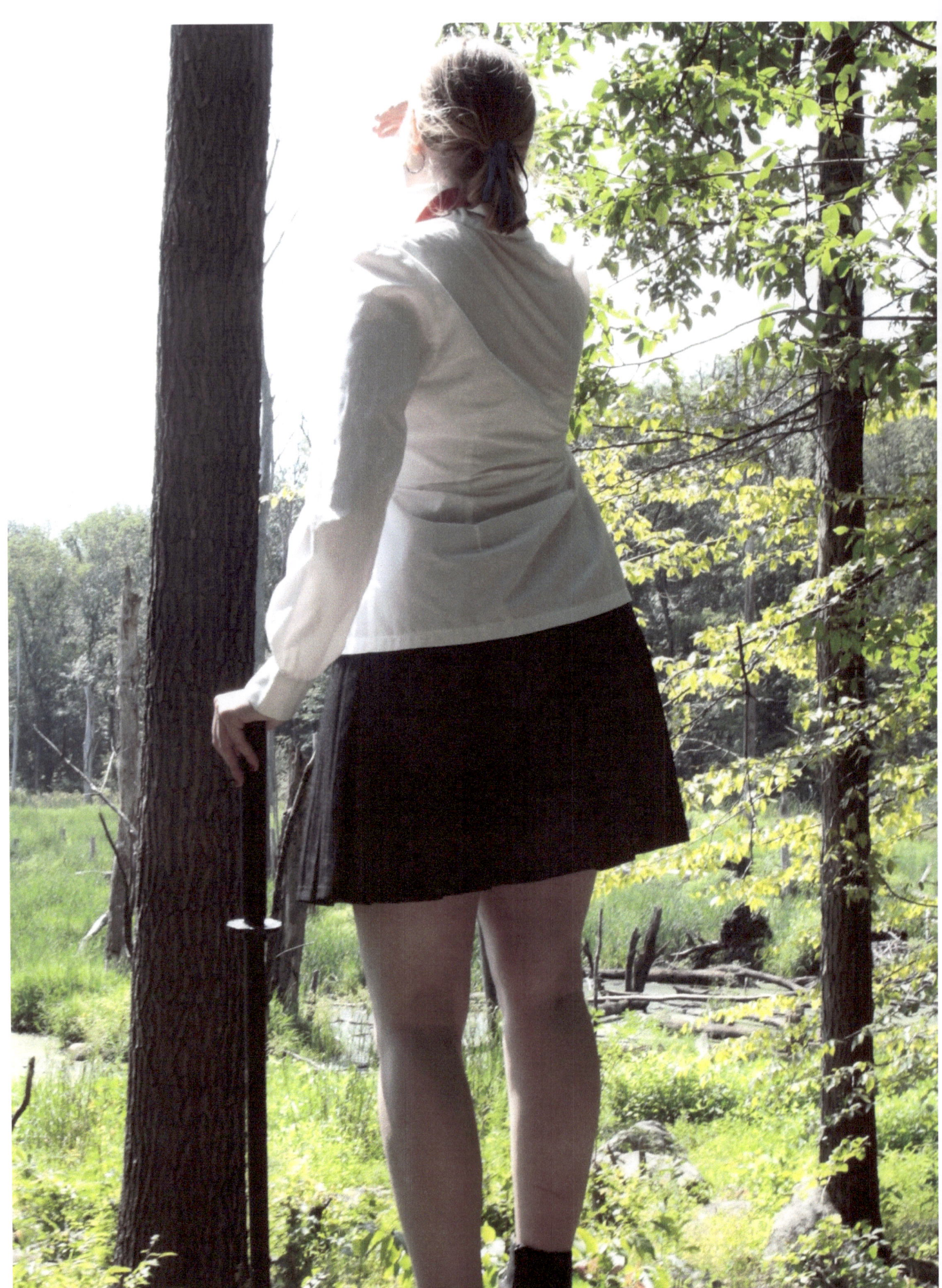

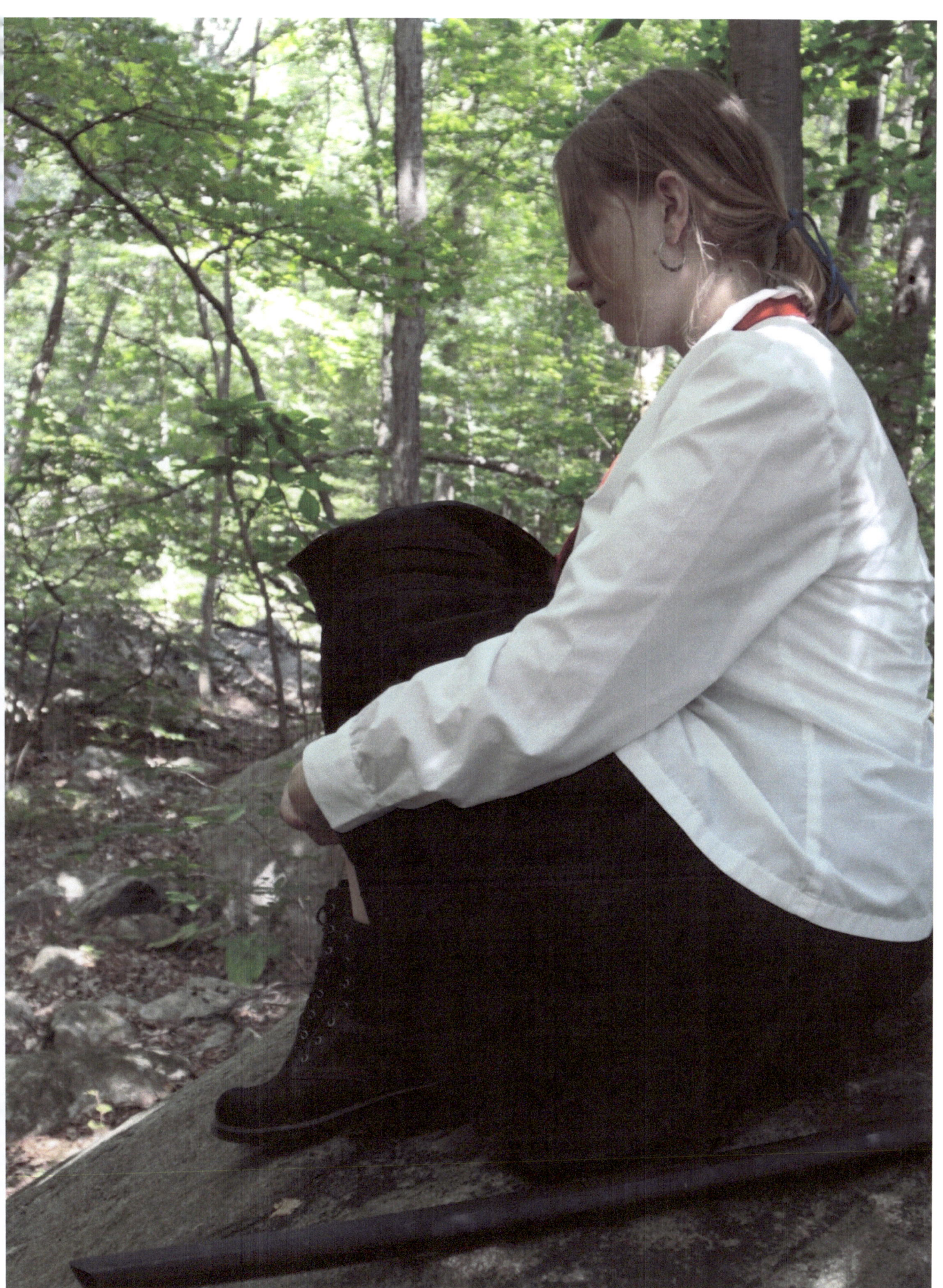

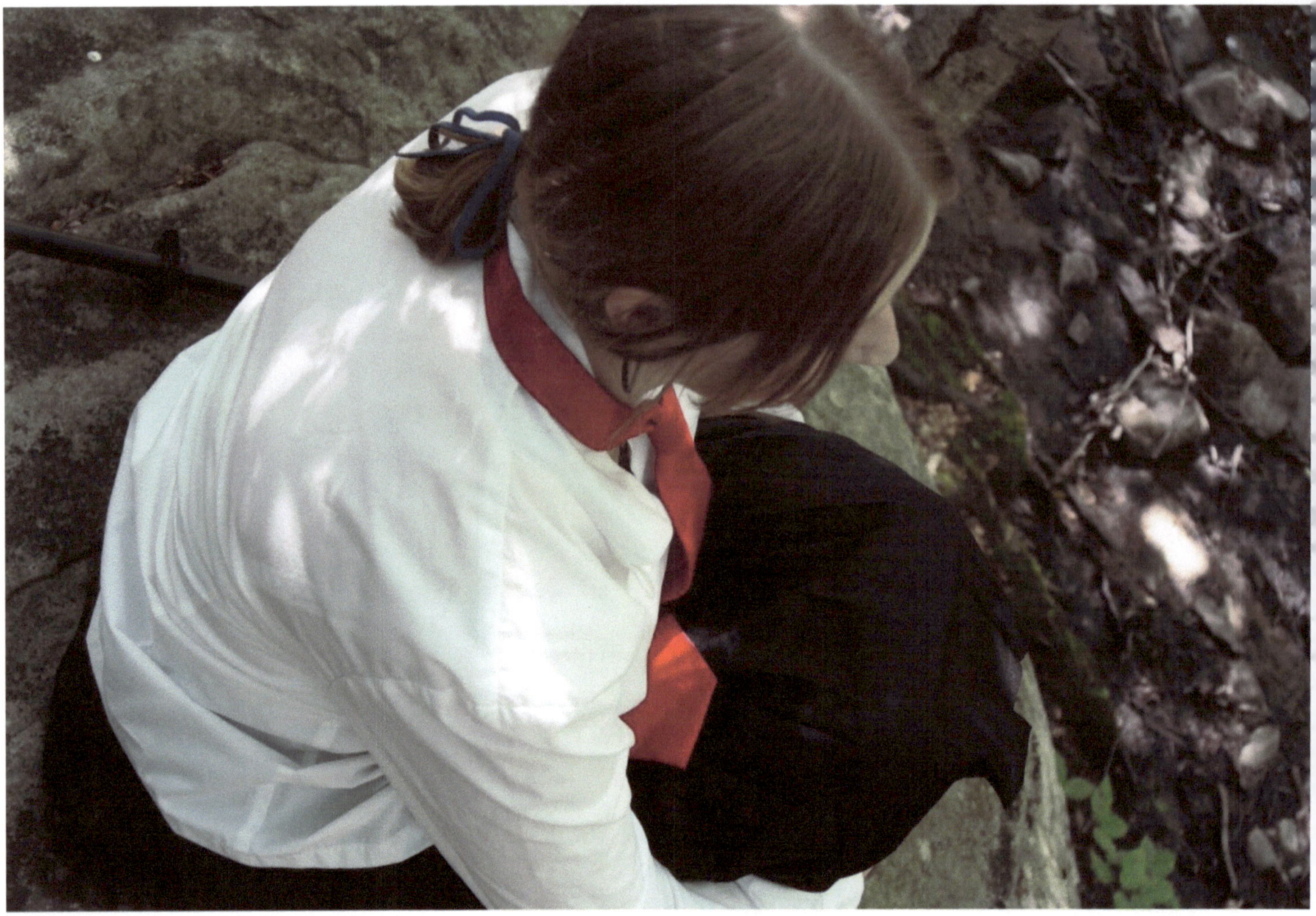

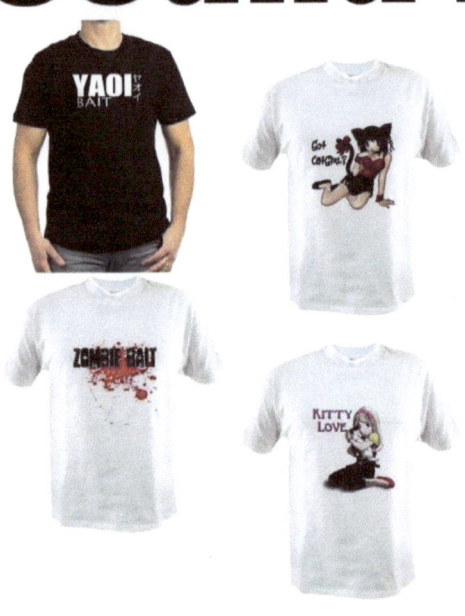
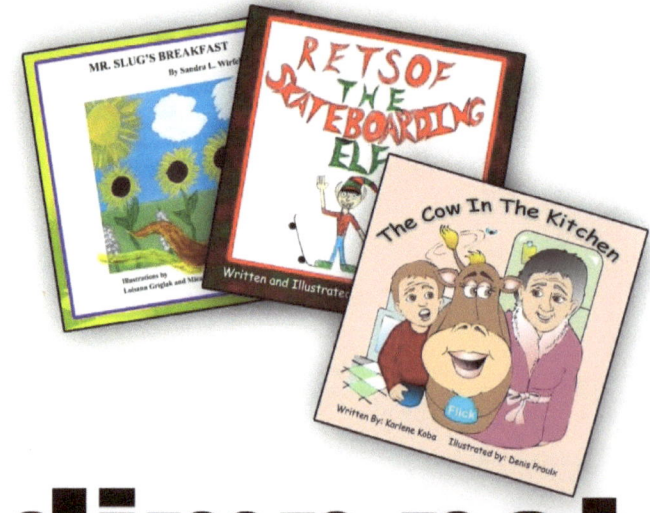